A SCHOOL OF OUR OWN

Also by Susan Engel

The End of the Rainbow: How Educating for Happiness (Not Money)
Would Transform Our Schools

The Hungry Mind: The Origins of Curiosity in Childhood

Real Kids: Making Meaning in Everyday Life

The Stories Children Tell: Making Sense of the Narratives of Childhood

Context Is Everything: The Nature of Memory

Red Flags or Red Herrings? Predicting Who Your Child Will Become

A SCHOOL OF OUR OWN

THE STORY OF THE FIRST STUDENT-RUN HIGH SCHOOL AND A NEW VISION FOR AMERICAN EDUCATION

Samuel Levin and Susan Engel

THE NEW PRESS

NEW YORK
LONDON

Requests for permission to reproduce selections from this book should be mailed to:
Permissions Department, The New Press, 120 Wall Street, 31st floor, New York, NY
10005.

Published in the United States by The New Press, New York, 2016
Distributed by Perseus Distribution

ISBN 978-1-62097-152-9 (hc)
ISBN 978-1-62097-153-6 (e-book)
CIP data is available.

The New Press publishes books that promote and enrich public discussion and
understanding of the issues vital to our democracy and to a more equitable world. These
books are made possible by the enthusiasm of our readers; the support of a committed
group of donors, large and small; the collaboration of our many partners in the
independent media and the not-for-profit sector; booksellers, who often hand-sell
New Press books; librarians; and above all by our authors.

www.thenewpress.com

Book design and composition by Bookbright Media
This book was set in Janson Text and Gill Sans

Printed in the United States of America

10 9 8 7 6 5 4 3 2 1

For Mr. P and the original Indies

CONTENTS

ACKNOWLEDGMENTS

Sam thanks Beth Denham for support and feedback every step of the way. Susan thanks her Williams students for their wonderful questions, ideas, and stories.

We both thank Marc Favreau for his love of books and education.

A SCHOOL OF OUR OWN

INTRODUCTION

High school isn't so bad. But when it comes to educating the next generation, not so bad is terrible. It has become something like a waiting room at a train station, a place for kids to hang out and pass the time on their way to somewhere else ostensibly more important, desirable, and interesting—adulthood. It is necessary, but not especially appealing or meaningful in its own right. For some teens, it's an abysmal waiting room—uncomfortable, tedious, and pointless. For others, the waiting room is perfectly nice—they spend their four years doing well on tests, passing the time with buddies, and serving on the student council. But for most, the waiting room is merely tolerable. And there's been too little talk about those kids.

We've been distracted by the extremes: kids who are so miserable in high school that they drop out, kill themselves, or get in legal trouble, or kids who thrive against all odds, working their way from poverty to great accomplishment.

But such vivid narratives of anguish and victory obscure the most common stories of all—the stories of the students who stay in school all four years, perhaps lucking into a good class every term or so, earning decent grades, keeping their heads down until college. These students seem okay. No triumph, no tragedy. But they are simply enduring school, thinking about what comes next, and waiting till it's over. For most kids in this country, high school is, at best, mediocre.

Listening to teens and adults talk about high school, you would think it was inevitable for teenagers to spend four of the most important and vibrant years of their lives simply getting by.

The truth is, we know from a wealth of recent research that adolescence is a volatile and potent developmental moment in a person's life. As Laurence Steinberg, a leading expert on adolescence, says, it's the age of psychological opportunity. Sometime between the ages of thirteen and fourteen, teenagers achieve new heights of intellectual ability, explode with interest in the world around them, and begin relating to others in ways they weren't able to before. They also are still cognitively flexible and receptive, intellectually and morally hungry, able to learn complex material, and filled with energy, a kind that won't last beyond early adulthood. In other words, they have developmentally unique strengths and capacities. And yet, high school seems to make no use of all that potential.

Is there any inherent reason why teenagers in our culture must spend the bulk of their time in settings that are confining, rigid, ugly, and disconnected from their communities, doing tasks that feel (and often are) pointless, devoid of meaning, and irrelevant to the things that most concern them?

We don't think so. One of us (Susan) is a developmental psychologist who has spent the last thirty-five years studying the paths by which children become adults and trying to figure out how schools can optimize rather than subvert children's personal growth. The other (Sam) actually did it. When he was sixteen years old, Sam started a new kind of high school, the Independent Project, a school within a public school in western Massachusetts. It succeeded beyond expectations, and in unpredictable ways.

The school he founded was based on a few simple ideas about what kids are like, what they need, what they are capable of, and what they should get out of their high school experience. Though the ideas are simple, they are strikingly different from what you see in most schools throughout the country. Moreover, they are slippery: straightforward but easy to get wrong.

We wrote this book together because the idea of the Independent

Project grew out of conversations between us. As the school came to life, we continued having conversations: about the ideas themselves, about how to embody those ideas in specific educational practices, and about what was working and what wasn't. Susan talked to Sam about educational theory and the psychology of adolescence, and Sam talked to Susan about what he and his friends yearned for at school.

Here we were, a teacher and a student, a mother in her fifties and a young man in his teens, someone who had thought endlessly about schools and someone who started one—both of us eager to put *theory* and *practice* together.

Because we played such different roles in the creation of the Independent Project, and because we come to the whole enterprise from two vantage points, we thought it essential that we each tell our part of the story in our own way, one from the inside and one from the outside. Because our thinking about schools over the last few years has been a constant dialogue, the book follows suit. We alternate between Susan's voice and Sam's.

There's one more reason we wrote this book together. In addition to being teacher and student, older and younger, psychologist and adolescent, we are also mother and son. The school, and the argument that emerged, began at our dinner table.

The book contains three interwoven threads. First, a new idea about teenagers and education. This idea draws on research and theory. But it also draws on the everyday experiences of kids, parents, and teachers who live high school day in and day out.

It is also the story of the Independent Project: what it took to start a new school in a public school district, who those first students were, and what happened to them; their missteps, their crises, and their victories.

Finally, it is a guide for those who want to start their own schools. And "those" doesn't mean just grown-ups. We think teenagers should have a hand in shaping their own education. This book isn't just for school administrators. It's for everyone—parents, teachers, high schoolers. We feel that the core features of the Independent Project solve some important problems with our current educational system, and so we have provided a guide for re-creating it.

Each chapter of the book is a step in the process of building a school. There are eight chapters and eight steps. If you follow them, then at the end of this book you will have a blueprint for your own new school. Each chapter follows the story of the Independent Project, from inception to present day. Throughout, Susan tells her parts of the story and Sam tells his.* Each chapter is also a manifesto of sorts, an exegesis of the way in which we think high schools could better serve their students.

Three threads, two authors, one school.

---

* Susan's is in one typeface, Sam's in another, and italics are used, often at the beginning and ends of chapters, when they are speaking together.

REALIZE YOU NEED ONE

I was pissed off. It wasn't the first day I had come home from school feeling that way, but it would be one of the last. I was sixteen years old, and I had just started my junior year.

I was actually doing fine. My grades were good. Although a lot of my classes sucked, and I had a few teachers I hated, I also had a few I loved—teachers I could really connect to and learn from. And that was just about enough. After all, this had always been the case: mostly not very good teachers, mostly quite boring classes, but one or two life preservers to keep me afloat.

And I suppose it wasn't that big a deal. My days were, by and large, good. I usually woke up at 4:15 to the pitch black, rolled out of bed, and yanked on some blue jeans and a few layers of shirts. I went into the kitchen, turned on the coffee machine, and packed my backpack. Often my mom had made me a lunch the night before, but if not I would throw a sandwich together. Then I put the coffee in a jar with lots of milk and sugar, shoved on my Timberland boots, grabbed a pair of sneakers, and drove ten minutes to the dairy farm where I worked.

I loved the farm. I was usually the first one there, and I loved sliding open the big red doors on their rusty tracks as the first light crept into the day. I loved walking deep into the back fields to find the cows wherever they had been lurking in the night, and I loved walking them back inside, moving at their plodding pace. And I was lucky to have a great boss. He was demanding but understanding, a good teacher, knowledgeable, and really, really funny. I loved listening to NPR while we milked, almost as much as I loved the mornings (and there was no discerning what mornings they would be) when my boss decided we would work in silence.

Most of all, I loved the cows—their smell, the way the heat came off them in the cold barn (as I worked, I would slowly shed the layers I had started the day with). I even loved, for whatever twisted reason, the way Dame tried to kick me every time I milked her. Whenever there was a quiet moment in the barn, when I needed a rest, I would lean up against Freckles, our biggest steer, and relax against his warmth for a little while.

I worked as hard as I could there and loved every second of it. We milked, made cream, hayed the fields, cleaned the barn, stacked bales, moved the cows, cleaned the dairy room, fed the calves, moved the shit, and started again. I always left promptly at 7:30 a.m. Halfway to school I pulled off onto a dead-end dirt road, parked, took off my manure-covered boots, and put on my sneakers. If my pants were shit covered, and they often were, there was nothing I could do. I was lucky I had had the same friends my whole life, because there was no chance of making new friends smelling like cow crap every day.

I'd get to school before the first bell and park where my car was least likely to get keyed (a hangover from a brawl my friends and I had been involved in the year before). Then I'd sit through the first three periods of my day, mostly bored, occasionally annoyed. In the classes that were the least boring, I tried to think of ways to make them more interesting. I'd translate words to binary, think of alternative explanations for data that purported to support a theory, design math puzzles. In the most boring classes, I just thought about other things. I planned science experiments, wrote stories, or daydreamed. During chemistry class I wrote a speech that I would later deliver to ten thousand farmers and chefs.

Then, in period four, I had a one-on-one math class with my favorite teacher. She was a brilliant mathematician, excited, enthusiastic, humble, and quick to admit what she didn't know. We'd cram as much math into the forty minutes allotted to us as we could. We'd search for better and better math books, more and more interesting puzzles, try our hand at original proofs, and then the bell would ring, always a few minutes too soon.

Lunch meant hanging out with my friends, on the lawn if it was sunny. That was also always too short—never enough time to complete our prank or hear Red's* joke or slip into town to get doughnuts—but messing around with the guys provided fuel for the rest of the day.

After lunch was English, which was so bad it wasn't boring. I usually got too infuriated to be bored. I argued endlessly with my teacher, who seemed to not like books, or kids for that matter. The kids thing bothered me a little, the books thing a lot.

I can't remember the last two periods. And then the final bell would ring. The next three hours of my time would be spent at school (not playing basketball or baseball—I had already given those up by junior year—but I'll get to those three hours later), and then I'd drive home. The first thing I'd do was go down into the basement, where I had constructed a makeshift lab. I had four lentic water tanks and one river tank, which I had bought with money from a grant I had won the year before. One of these tanks was usually covered by a black cloth; the others were under bright lights. The tanks were occupied by caddisfly larvae, on which I was experimenting. I'd spend an hour doing what needed to be done—dissecting the larval cases, marking the individual caddisflies, photographing their constructions, blinding them, and so on. And then it was dinner, and then a couple of hours of homework, and then some *Simpsons* before bed with a glass of water and a good Stephen King novel.

So I guess you could say I didn't have that much to be upset about. Sure, there were long stretches of boredom in my day, and several moments of frustration, but there was also the farm in the morning, that

---

* The people and situations in this book are real, but we have changed the names for the sake of privacy.

stellar math class to break up my day, and the larvae awaiting me in the basement at home. Who was I to complain? I should have been happy, or at least content, but certainly not pissed off.

And yet, by the time I came home that day, I was furious. That's because it wasn't just about me. It was everyone else. It was what I saw all around me.

By the time Sam was in eleventh grade, his older brothers, Jake and Will, had finished college. I knew how easy it was to think teenagers needed a guiding hand at every turn. I had watched, intruded, kibitzed, meddled, admired, fretted, and engineered as they groped their way from puberty to adulthood. Part of this came from the fact that it was hard to step back from the kind of constant care younger children need. It took me a kid or two to get comfortable with my new role. But it was also true that I was painfully aware, like other parents, of the pit-falls of adolescence. After all, there are so many ways for kids between the ages of fourteen and eighteen to screw up. It would be hard not to quake at the potential disasters that lie in wait for the teen who goes astray. Many parents and teachers in our culture have a deeply rooted sense that if we let go of the reins for more than an hour, our teenage children will lose their homework, get a bad grade, stay out too late, have sex without a condom, make the wrong friend, drop out, turn to drugs, waste their time, get bad test scores, not get into college, and before you know it become homeless and jobless. In other words, all hell will break loose. Which may explain why we've drawn tighter and tighter circles around high school students.

The paradox here is that most parents and teachers readily agree that by the time our kids are somewhere around twenty years old, it's imperative that they can make wise decisions, use their time well, choose worthwhile pursuits, and take good care of themselves. In other words, we want them to be independent. Yet, strangely, as Sam began to notice during his junior year, we want them to acquire all of those skills without giving them much practice at any of it while they are in school.

In *Patterns of Culture*, the anthropologist Ruth Benedict noted that many cultures lead their youngsters toward maturity by gradually giving them more autonomy and accountability. But our culture, she pointed out, did not. In fact, she argued, our society was notable for the disjuncture we create between childhood and adulthood. We baby them for a very long time and then fling them into a free fall toward adulthood.

That's just as true today as it was when Benedict wrote her book, in 1934. We tell kids what to do every moment they are in school. We don't even trust them to keep track of time, ringing a bell whenever they should get up and begin moving to the next class. If you've spent time in a public school, you'll know what I mean. The students sit, slouch, or fidget in their seats. Then suddenly, from nowhere, a loud, ugly chime sounds, and everyone jumps up (even when the teacher or another student is still talking, or a film is showing), puts their books in their backpacks, and begins shuffling toward the door. There is absolutely no decision making involved. They each begin moving, like sardines on the conveyer belt, toward their next destination, another classroom in another hall.

And it's not just their time we control. We tell them what to learn as well. For the most part adults decide what topics are essential to study, what books they should read, which math they should learn, and what kinds of experiments they should conduct. Teenagers are typically treated as if they have no clue how to choose what to apply themselves to, what they are interested in, or how to go about pursuing those interests. We also tell them how to learn the topics we have selected: what material they should study, which skills to practice, and the best way to prepare for a test. We even relieve them of any responsibility for deciding when they actually know something well enough. Instead, we tell them, usually with a test score.

Yet suddenly, when they hit their eighteenth birthday, everything changes. By then we have given them license to drive a lethal weapon and smoke as much as they want and have invited them to help select the nation's president. During times of war, we send them off to protect us, to kill, and to make life-and-death decisions, all in a foreign country.

We expect them to make a decision that will shape the rest of their lives by choosing college, work, or the army. Now they can get married if they want to. Last but not least, having kept them powerless long beyond puberty, we demand that they quickly become self-supporting. We ask them to leap from childhood into adulthood. But of course, though our society treats this transition as a leap, the truth is teenagers don't leap: they stumble, jump, skip, slide, and trudge their way into maturity.

In describing this gradual and winding path toward maturity, the psychologist Kurt Lewin said that the teenager was "the marginal man," standing outside, caught between two worlds. Teenagers have left the pleasures and freedom of childhood behind but do not yet have the responsibilities or autonomy of adulthood. It takes time to travel this sometimes circuitous and often difficult route. Yet our high schools have functioned less like a path from dependence to independence and more like a holding pen with a diving board at the exit gate.

This immobilizing has other bad consequences. By directing them through every waking moment, we all but guarantee that they are unlikely to feel much zeal or drive for what they are learning and trying to do. In the early 1980s the psychologists Mihaly Csikszentmihalyi and Reed Larson wanted to get a detailed, vivid picture of adolescent experience. They gave teenagers in Chicago small beepers to take with them everywhere, and a packet of questionnaires. For more than a week, each teenager in the study was beeped at random times. When the subjects in the study heard the beep, they would take a moment to pause and answer a host of questions about where they were, what they were doing, who they were with, what they were thinking about, and how they felt (they had a chance even to sketch pictures of their moods). The study offered a gold mine of information about how teenagers spent their time and, more important, provided an amazingly intimate and gritty picture of what it felt like to be a teenager. The answers made it vividly clear that most kids feel listless and disengaged for most of the school day. But there were places and times during the school day when the opposite was true—when kids reported a sense of focus, energy, and excitement about what they were doing. When did those moments occur? When the students were doing things they had chosen: whether it was during a class or not, kids felt much more alive when they had some say in their activity. Sadly, however, these moments were the exception, not the rule.

What I saw around me, what made me so mad, was that most of my friends were struggling. Many of them were getting bad grades. Sometimes it was because the work was too challenging. But most of the time it wasn't. They didn't care about anything they were learning. They weren't engaged in their classes, because the subject matter often seemed dry, boring, irrelevant, and unrelated to them. And this meant that when they got home, they would usually choose hiking, basketball, making out with their girlfriends, or reading good books over anatomy homework. And I didn't blame them. Most of what we were learning *was* boring. Or even if the subject matter itself was interesting, the way we learned it turned it into something lifeless and dull. I'd sit in class thinking about how vapid geometry was. Then, at home, I'd read a book in which the characters were shapes discovering other dimensions, and I'd become totally enthralled. But I'd grow annoyed at the same time, knowing that my friends wouldn't get a chance to have the same experience. They'd just go on struggling to memorize the Pythagorean theorem.

Even worse, some of my friends *were* doing fine, doing really well even, but were just as disengaged as the friends who were struggling. The problem was, the nature of most of our classes meant that you could learn the material well enough to get good grades without ever really engaging with it in any meaningful way. We would learn the periodic table—something I now know to be elegant and fascinating—by memorizing the abbreviations and their places in the boxes. So you could sail by on a test without ever knowing how the periodic table might save lives, or how you would use it to go about designing an experiment to find a new element. So the friends who were getting straight As were doing it without ever becoming passionate about their work or about learning itself.

The truth is, no one liked school, or at least not the part of school that was supposed to be education. And the result was that pretty much everyone around me was unhappy. Maybe this sounds perfectly normal, like school isn't supposed to be something kids enjoy. But why? We go to school not just once or twice a year, but seven hours a day, 180 days a year. Why should kids be unhappy so much of the time? Maybe if all of my friends were becoming really thoughtful, enlightened, well-educated people, I might have overlooked the unhappiness (maybe). But that wasn't the case at all. No one was learning anything either. It was all intertwined—the disengagement, the unhappiness, the lack of real learning—and it all tied together in a vicious feedback loop.

Nothing unusual happened that day, sometime in September of 2009, when I came home pissed off. It was as good and as bad and as banal as the other days. I went to the farm, Dame tried to kick me; I sat through several boring lessons, had a great argument with my math teacher about prime numbers, had a bad argument with my English teacher about the merit of excerpts, and eventually came home and changed the water in my aquariums. There was no sudden outrage, no particular offense. But clearly it had been slowly accumulating, like a poison leaking into my system, all the letdowns, all the frustrations, all the disappointments, all the failures of our system, and, most of all, all the misery around me. It was all swirling around in my head as I drove home from school.

And when I sat down at the dinner table with my mom, all that frustration just burst out of me. "Mom, I'm sick and tired of my friends being unhappy in school," I said, my head in my hands. "I'm sick of my friends not learning, sick of them being disengaged. So much of the way school does things doesn't make sense. I can't take it anymore." Like I said, it wasn't the first time I had come home feeling that way, and it wasn't the first time I had vocalized these feelings either. Even if there was a little more venom in my voice this time, she had heard it all before. Which is why, perhaps, I was surprised by how she responded.

*   *   *

When Sam came home with a black cloud hovering over his face, at first I barely noticed. I had spent more than twenty years sitting at that same kitchen table, listening to my kids tell me about their school days. Each afternoon, as the light faded from the sky, my sons would sit down while I cooked and recount their highs and lows. I would hear tales of woe (a Halloween costume outlawed by the school, an unfairly graded paper, a missed shot in basketball, a bad rumor about a girlfriend) and tales of triumph (beating a team from a richer town, acing a test, a prom date with the elusive girl, a poem that garnered praise from a beloved teacher).

My husband and I had sent all three of our sons to the local public schools in western Massachusetts, where we live. They had spelling tests, book reports, recess, concerts, and tedious homework. The usual stuff. Lots of it seemed fine. There were disappointments and frustrations, missed opportunities and bad teaching, but nothing that seemed particularly outrageous. It's the stuff most families endure.

When my eldest son, Jake, was in seventh grade, all the students were told to plan projects that would take several months, something that would demonstrate their skill and effort. They were given wide leeway. It seemed great. Jake chose to study a new translation of the *Odyssey* and make clay tiles depicting several of his favorite stories. He used an ancient technique for glazing the tiles and retold sections of each story on aged paper, written in calligraphy he learned to do for the project. When his tiles went up in the big gym along with all the other student projects (a boat, a birdhouse, a fashion show), his grade was marked down—not colorful enough, the teachers said. When he walked in the door and mentioned this, my ears began burning. I was thinking, "What? This project is bursting with scholarship! He's twelve and he chose the *Odyssey*. *Are you kidding me?* 'Needs more color'?"

But I didn't say any of that out loud. I just shook my head and said, "Well, honey, we love it. Let's hang it on the wall." I put the incident aside. After all, I thought, he was lucky to be in a school that gave students the chance to do projects. And Jake was a school lover. He wanted to make every assignment as interesting as possible. Each assignment was a fresh chance to throw himself into something, whether he clashed with the teacher or not. I wasn't worried about it. He was learning to stand up for his ideals, I thought.

Jake's younger brother Will had a whole other kind of high school experience. He was brimming with a different kind of strength and energy. Watching him, I saw how a charismatic and talented kid could navigate his way through high school unscathed. Agile in mind and body, he could get through the whole four years with great grades yet was wonderfully untouched by formal academics.

For Will, classes were something like a virus, something to keep at arm's length. When he was good at something (languages, philosophy, math), he did his schoolwork with pleasure and ease. But he was economical with his time—he did the least amount of work possible to get a good grade. He had other more captivating things to do. He found all of his fun in the parking lot (lifting a teacher's car with some friends and carrying it to another parking spot), on the basketball court, and in the hallways, offering sidesplitting imitations of other students or teachers being ridiculous. As he progressed through high school, he found fewer and fewer teachers to connect to, and more and more of the school day seemed a chore to be finished as quickly as possible. I told myself that it was fine if he spent seven hours a day stifled and bored, drumming his fingers and watching the clock, as long as he came to life when it was time for basketball practice.

And then there was Sam. From day one, he seemed made for school. He liked spelling bees, math projects, lunchtime, and running for class president. What was not to like? And yet he, too, collected his share of frustrations, and they seemed to mount as time went on.

In eighth grade he collided with an English teacher. They had read a Rod Serling story: "The Monsters Are Due on Maple Street." He interpreted the story one way, she another. She told him he was just dead wrong, that maybe he'd understand the next story better. They were assigned to write a biography of Dr. Seuss, and he wrote his in verse. The teacher told him not to get carried away with rhymes. One year he found science class so dull he spent his time trying to mentally suss out the origins of various Latinate words. By March he had a full glossary.

Looking back now, I can see that, though he loved school, by the time he was twelve, he had begun to chafe against all the arbitrary rules and empty academic conventions. He was an ebullient kid, irrepressible. He couldn't accept the limits they kept placing on him. When his middle school principal reprimanded him for putting an arm around a buddy who had just lost an important soccer game ("No physical contact allowed in the halls," she said), he considered bringing a suit of discrimination against the school: "Mom, what if we were gay? Wasn't that homophobia?"

But for a long time, each story of a disappointing conversation with a teacher, a rule that hindered rather than helped learning, or of assignments that were outrageously superficial seemed like the ordinary obstacles that teenagers stumble over in school. I wasn't worried. There was so much of value in public schools—people from all walks of life, baseball and concerts that brought families together, now and then a great French or history teacher, a cool project painting murals, and every once in a while a wonderful book or really interesting paper topic. My kids were fine.

So when Sam walked in that gloomy fall day, sat down at the kitchen table with a frustrated, grim look on his face, and said, "I can't take it anymore," I was tempted to offer a glib and seemingly obvious answer. I wanted to say, "They're teenagers, hon. Of course they're bored and apathetic. That's their job." That was the developmental psychologist in me talking. I've read more studies that I can count providing biological and psychological evidence explaining why teenagers are inherently dissatisfied, mercurial, and defiant.

But his normally blue eyes looked so gray and stormy. And suddenly, a switch flipped in my head. All those many snapshots I had stored about school—small disappointments, assignments that were just a little less than they should be, rules that prevented rather than encouraged teenagers to blossom, lost opportunities—came flooding back into my mind. My old story, that school was good enough, that the

pluses outweighed the minuses, that the obstacles were part of the experience, didn't really make sense. The pictures hadn't changed. I didn't
remember all those vignettes differently. But sitting there I realized that
they told a different story than the one I had been carrying around in
my head for twenty years. The small grievances were no longer just
aggravating obstacles—they were the fabric that shaped four pivotal
years in adolescents' development. In the new story, which rapidly unfolded in my mind that day, teenagers' best, most potent qualities were
persistently pushed aside or neglected, over and over again. What had
seemed to be a long line of unrelated and relatively minor mistakes
now seemed to reveal something deeper and off base about the whole
structure. That day I realized that high schools are suited in almost no
way to what teens are like, or what they really need.

At that moment I knew Sam was right to be outraged. The turbulent
look in his eyes suddenly meant something more than just reasonable
frustration that should and would pass. And before I had a second to
reconsider, the next words just popped out of my mouth: "Then why
don't you start your own school?"

And I guess the story could end there. I could have laughed, then
sighed, then fixed up a bowl of cereal. Or maybe made some joke, like,
"Yeah, one day, Mom, when I rule the world." Lots of people feel sick
and tired sometimes; it's a part of life. And there was no reason why
I would expect anything to change. The public school system hadn't
changed much since it was created during the industrial revolution.
So I could have accepted that that was the way it was—after all, I was
a junior, which meant only two more years of feeling sick and tired.

Except. Except that I knew better. I knew that it didn't *have* to be
this way. I knew that high schoolers *could be* enormously engaged, passionate, motivated, and committed. I knew that they were capable of
being ferocious learners and workers. I knew that they had almost limitless potential. And I knew all this because much of the last three
years of my life had been spent in a garden.

When I was a freshman in high school, in 2007, I had a really simple idea: I would build a garden at my school. It would be run by students and it would grow food for the cafeterias. Less of our food would be coming from far away, reducing our school's carbon footprint. Students who ate food from a garden they could see would start thinking about where their food came from and would become more connected to the land. Those who worked in the garden would start to care for the natural world. And if I was lucky, teachers in the school district would start using the garden as an outdoor classroom.

Not knowing who would be the best person to talk to about my idea, I went to my guidance counselor, Joe Huron, and said, "I want to start a garden." I was only fourteen and hadn't experienced more than a few weeks of high school. So at the time, his response seemed absolutely normal, just what every counselor would say. He said, "Okay, what do you need from me?"

I told him a bit more about my idea, and after a little while he said, "Wait here," and left the office. Five minutes later, he walked in with two older girls—a sophomore named Lily and a junior named Rosa— whom he had just pulled from class. He knew that they had also been talking about getting local, organic food into the cafeteria. He thought maybe we could work together.

Within half an hour, the idea of Project Sprout was born. The three of us agreed that a garden that provided both education and food to the schools was the thing to do. It all seemed very straightforward. We lived in a rural area, and the school had plenty of land. They could just hand some of it over!

Of course, it wasn't that easy. To the administration, the idea of handing over a plot of land to a bunch fourteen- and fifteen-year-olds was ludicrous. It would be a disaster, they thought (and often said). We would dig up some beautiful stretch of lawn, lose interest, and move on to our next fancy (probably a new video game), and the school would have to pay to clean up our mess (not to mention the embarrassment!).

But our hearts were set. We weren't about to give up. So we spent six months planning, pitching, arguing, designing, pulling, and prodding, and eventually the School Committee agreed to let us build a small, thousand-square-foot garden on an old soccer field across the street from the high school. It would be a trial year. If we really followed through (they said, secretly rolling their eyes), we could propose doing it a second year.

What they didn't realize, what even I didn't fully grasp, was what can happen when you let a bunch of high schoolers pursue something they are passionate about. The garden wasn't successful in spite of being completely run by students. It was successful *because* students ran it. By the time I left high school, we had a twelve-thousand-square-foot vegetable plot, plus hundreds of berry plants, an orchard, two sheds, a farm stand, and a greenhouse. In four years we raised more than $100,000. We planned events for hundreds of people at a time, started delivering vegetables to three schools in our district three days a week, and had hundreds of classes and after-school programs taught in the garden—which, by the time I was a junior, was really more of a farm.

The evening Sam walked in churned up about his high school friends was not, by a long shot, the first time he had burst through the door practically levitating with a feeling or a thought. Even as a baby, Sam's reactions had been intense. He startled easily as an infant, and when really upset, he'd open his mouth and take such a long pause for the cry to emerge that he'd periodically lose consciousness for a second. Even at four months, he was a man of conviction. When he was two he tried to peer under a large rock to watch the worms that lay in the dirt beneath. But his fat little hands couldn't hold the rock, and it fell, smashing his foot, turning his stubby little toes to chopped meat. The orthopedist, looking at his tiny damaged foot, said Sam should really be on crutches for a brief time, if only a toddler could manage such a thing. Sam's face lit up. Yes, he wanted them! The hospital provided him with teensy-weensy crutches, with which he tore around the house at fever pitch for the next two weeks. The foot pain was nothing compared to the thrill of the crutches.

So I wasn't particularly surprised when Sam flopped down on our couch one afternoon in the winter of his freshman year and said, "Guess what! We're gonna start an organic garden. We're gonna feed the school district." "Nice, sweetie pie," I said. "That's a lovely idea. Honey"—his grandfather, a farmer, who had died the year before—"would be so proud. Do you have homework tonight, or you gonna watch TV with me?" Then he said, "The team is coming tomorrow to spend the day planning. Can you get some stuff for me to serve at lunch so that we can work straight through? And can we have the whole living room? We have a lot of things to figure out."

In the days and weeks that followed I learned that the day did not hold twenty-four hours, but instead about thirty-two: eight for sleep, eight for school, two for sports, two for homework, two for eating and posting messages on Facebook, and presto, somehow always another ten for planning his garden.

Finally, I realized, Sam had stumbled upon something big enough, captivating enough, and complex enough to absorb him fully—something that he woke up thinking about and fell asleep thinking about. Something of his own. He still liked some of his classes, and, at least at first, he still liked being on the baseball and basketball teams. But all of that, really, was just background to the garden. In all of those he was an actor in someone else's drama. He was the student writing a paper someone else had thought of, a point guard following the coach's play.

But in the garden, he and the other kids were the writers, the directors, the actors, and the stagehands. And believe me, there was plenty of drama in this drama. There were kids who didn't show up for important meetings, fights about how big the first plot of tilled land should be, about how much help to get from the adults, and about whether they could or should feature a spit-fired pig at their first fund-raiser.

Every decision seemed crucial, every detail important. Sam had never once asked me for help on a piece of schoolwork. But when it came to the garden, he pressed hard and constantly. Could I rent a rototiller and deliver it to the land? Could I take him to the printers to have the posters made? Could I make sure he got to the garden by 5 a.m. so that he could water early? Could he borrow all of our rakes and hoes so that the fourth grade could come help clear between the rows? Could I just spend a few days making pesto with all the leftover basil? Could he use my cell phone as I drove him to baseball practice so that he could call a farmer and make sure the pig would be big enough by the day of their benefit? Could I swing by the fabric outlet and pick up the T-shirts they had designed and commissioned?

But it wasn't just my own kid who seemed so thrillingly maxed out. That first May when the kids held their fund-raiser (and yes, it featured a whole pig, turning on a spit), I showed up nervously at noon, the start time. I had told myself again and again that even if only the families of the core team were there, that would be about twenty people. And what a great day we'd have, eating pig and potato salad, proud of our kids for trying this. The first thing I saw was a group of the A-wingers, so named because they took most of their classes in the vocational wing, or A-wing, of the school and were known as the lower ability, or less academic students. They were dressed in matching green Project Sprout T-shirts, happily, politely, and skillfully showing us where to park. And there beyond, under a tent, I saw another twenty kids, also in their green Project Sprout T-shirts, serving the food they had spent days preparing, to two hundred guests. I had seen all of these kids over the past six years, loping, lounging, scowling through the hallways. Often when I had passed them in classes or during a school event, they were gazing out the window or sitting slumped in their seats, watching their teachers with half-lidded eyes. These same kids, now a sea of green, looked so different. They were bounding around the parking lot, clear and certain about how to pack the cars in and get the guests to the tent. They looked excited to see that so many people had showed up. The ones serving food were explaining in cheerful voices where the potatoes in the potato salad came from and how the rhubarb had been harvested. They were calling out instructions to one another ("Bring out the extra pies"; "Yeah, the nettles need to be stirred"). Though every single one of those teenagers was familiar to me, they now looked different. And the truth is, they were.

*   *   *

So it was the garden that served as my breaking point. Because it was there that I saw the true potential of high schoolers, there that I saw what we were really missing in school.

Here's what I saw. One spring, we got behind schedule building the beds for the garden. The seedlings that we had started in the greenhouse needed to be in the ground by the end of May, as did our first seeds. It was the start of the first weekend in May, and we hadn't built a single bed. So we had three weeks to build 150 beds, on top of all the other fund-raising and planning we were doing. Even for us, that was unrealistic.

One Friday afternoon, as we were leaving school, I told Adrian, my buddy and fellow gardener, how I felt. I was frustrated, and I was disappointed. "I can't see a way to get back on track," I told him.

"Well," he said, "I guess we only have one choice. Start digging."

So that's what we did. We went down to the garden and started working on a bed. At some point, a car pulled up, one I didn't recognize and certainly hadn't seen at the garden before. The door opened, and out hopped Riley McLaughlin, a popular soccer player at our school. I was surprised to see him there—not his usual territory—and figured he needed a favor or something.

Instead, he said he wanted to help. "Track was canceled today, so I don't have anything to do until my doctor's appointment in a couple of hours," he told us. "I thought I'd lend a hand." We told him thanks, but it was fine, we weren't really having a workday. "Got nothin' else to do!" he said.

So we handed him a shovel and explained how to build a bed, and he started digging.

But at some point Adrian and I remembered we had to pick up the posters for our upcoming event before the print shop closed. We told Riley we had to leave, and I went to grab his shovel.

"You know, if you don't mind," said Riley, "I'll just keep digging for a bit. It'll pass the time."

So we left him there, went to town, picked up the posters, and went for a coffee; the time passed, and we completely forgot about Riley. I think we both assumed he dug for another five minutes and left. But when we returned to the garden a few hours later, there was Riley, at the other end of the garden, head down, digging his tenth bed.

The next morning was Saturday, our community workday. There had been a big party the night before, so the volunteers were few and far between. "Oh well," I thought, "at least Riley got us a head start." We might even get twenty-five of our beds done, if we stayed late. But around 10 o'clock, Riley reappeared, and this time he brought the rest of track team, still in their uniforms, fresh from practice. I don't know when, but at some point I looked up and there were seven guys in base-ball uniforms too. Around noon I realized there were more people in the garden than there had been at the party the night before. An hour before our normal stop time, the 150th bed was finished, two weeks ahead of schedule.

The thing is, the kids who worked in the garden weren't paid, didn't get school credit, didn't get any external reward whatsoever for their work there. And yet, they woke up at 5:30 in the morning on school days to harvest for the cafeterias, stayed late after school, skipped holidays, and even gave up beloved sports to commit more of their time. They woke up at 7 a.m. every Saturday for community volunteer days. Saturday mornings! Nothing gets high schoolers up on Saturday mornings!

And that was it. That's what really started to wind me up. I began to wonder, why couldn't kids wake up at 7 on a Saturday morning to read Kafka, or do a science experiment, or solve a math puzzle?

Well, I began to think, maybe they could. I began to think that if high schoolers could shift mountains to grow a garden, they could do it for their education, too. But for that to happen, I knew some things had to change.

So the story doesn't end with me laughing and eating a bowl of cereal. Instead, when my mom said, "Why don't you start your own school?" there was a long silence at the dinner table. And then I said, "Okay, I will."

* * *

Sam's first step is your first step too. Come home one day and say, "This is not acceptable." Whether you're a student, parent, teacher, principal, or community member, starting a new high school begins with realizing you need one.

If the school you attend, the one your child attends, or the one where you teach is working well for most students (weak and strong, in-group and out-group, college bound and not), you don't need to read any further. You don't need a new school.

If you're a kid who dislikes school, one option is to put your head down and get through as best you can. Those of you who do well will tolerate the boredom and irrelevance and focus on getting really good grades so that you can get into a good college. If you are barely passing, or you get in trouble a lot, you can try hard to slip by. Look for easy courses, stay under the radar, and keep your eye on the calendar. Summer is not too far off. You, too, might not want to read further.

But, as a student, if you look around and realize that there are a lot of people your age who seem to have a huge amount of energy when they are doing things they care about with people they like, or are bursting with life when they are not at school, who have shown at some point (on the basketball court, in the soup kitchen, or at their weekend job downtown) that they are smart, capable, funny, and resourceful, but seem glazed over with boredom or submission when they are at school, you should consider starting a new school.

If you are a parent, teacher, or guidance counselor and you have seen how many young people seem to be biding their time, or working hard simply for the sake of future success, without any sense of meaning in their day, then you should encourage them to start a new school.

If your kid has ever come home with the same look of tumult and dissatisfaction as Sam had that day, then instead of just accepting that teenagers are stormy, consider that all of that passion and adolescent energy can be directed toward building something new.

The first step in starting a school is to realize that there is a need. All that means is that you think the young people in your community could be much more involved, much more engaged, and much more in charge than they are now. Don't wait for kids to say they want such a school. And don't wait for teachers or parents to say they are ready for something different. The idea may be so foreign to everyone that they can't even imagine something new. Some of the kids (and teachers) who ended up most loving the Independent Project didn't think it was right for them in the beginning.

If you've reached the end of this chapter, and you, too, feel like you've had enough with school being subpar, that there's a need for something better, then that's where you begin. But as we said at the start of this chapter, this is just the first step. Next, you must think long and hard about what a good school is made of.

2

DESIGN IT

You've realized you need a new school. What happens next? You need to design it. To be good, a new school has to build on an idea. If the first step came from paying close attention to what students (or teachers or parents) around you were feeling and thinking day in and day out, the second step requires you to stand back and think about what the goals of your school should be. You may want to ask others in the community what they think the purpose of a high school education is. You may read through the pages that follow and decide that our goals are your goals. But you must have a clear and vivid grasp of what an adolescent should experience or acquire at school.

This will allow you to come up with the specific activities, rituals, requirements, and opportunities you offer in your school. Without such thinking, you run the risk of repeating the same misguided practices that have been used and misused so many times in the past. You may come up with ideas that sound exciting or new, but have no real heft to them and don't lead anywhere intellectually or personally. Don't repeat mistakes, and don't do things that are simply novel or cute.

This is you thinking clearly and carefully about your idea. This is also you letting your mind wander and your imagination run wild.

The next nine months of my life were filled with endless discussions. I had decided to start a new school, and now I needed to design it. The best way I knew how to go about that was to talk to people.

Some of these discussions were with teachers: What do you find engages your students most? What do you wish you could do in your classroom but feel you're not allowed to? Some were with my friends: if you could change one thing about school, what would it be? But most of these conversations took place at the very same dinner table where it all started.

For the rest of my junior year, I would come home from school, sit down at the table, and talk to my mom about education. How should the day be structured? What should students spend their time doing? How much of it should they decide and how much should be woven into the fabric of the school? What role should teachers have?

Figuring out where to start was easy. I just thought about all the things that didn't make sense to me about the way things were being done in the current system, and then I thought about how I might change them to make them better.

The first, most glaring, most obvious thing missing from schools, it seemed to me, was autonomy. Students have absolutely no ownership over their own education, no real ability to choose what they learn or how they learn it. Sure, we got to choose a project here and there, or decide between modern Euro and American history, or between geometry and trig, but these are superficial choices, set within a fairly narrow and rigid box. You couldn't choose between math and ballet, sculpture and history. Further, within these courses, the curriculum was largely set in stone. Each assignment, direction, focus, topic was laid out in front of us like a set of Google Maps instructions. There was rarely, if ever, a sense that we were learning things that we had chosen to learn, or pursuing paths that interested us.

Something my best friend, James, said to me toward the end of that year really stuck with me. It was a Friday after school; the whole, unbroken, unfettered, glorious weekend spread out in front of us. We were sitting on the fire escape behind my dad's toy store, having an ice cream, planning out our night. Suddenly he turned to me and said, "Oh, by the way, I've been accepted to do a WISE project next year." WISE was a program at my school that allowed seniors to pursue a project, a high school thesis of sorts. Though I secretly hoped James would actually be one of the first students in my new school, at that point I still had no idea whether I'd ever actually have a new school.

"Cool," I said. "Congrats."

"It's crazy," he said, chomping down on his ice cream cone. "They said I can study whatever I want. I mean, really, I can learn *whatever* I want. How crazy is that?"

It seemed crazy, all right. But what really boggled my mind was that we could have an education system in which a seventeen-year-old feels like he's just discovered life on the moon when he has a chance to choose what he learns.

It made me want to find *THE PEOPLE IN CHARGE,* the all encompassing *THEY,* the ones who *MAKE DECISIONS,* grab them by the collar, and shout, "How can you ever expect me and my friends to learn if we aren't engaged? And how can you expect us to be engaged if we have no authority over what we are learning?"

But the choice—having a say over what we learned or how we learned it—wasn't the only thing that seemed out of whack about the lack of autonomy among high schoolers. Just as egregious, it seemed, was that students had no real responsibility in high school either. Say this to any high schooler—hell, say it to my sixteen-year-old self, and I would have just gawped at you. *No responsibility?* What about my endless homework assignments, my need to keep up my GPA, my college applications, the final exam?

But how sad, how frustrating, that this is what it means to have responsibility in high school. This isn't responsibility. At best, these are duties. If you pause to think about it, all the responsibility is really on the shoulders of the teachers. They decide what kids learn, how they learn it, how to measure whether they've actually learned it. It's their job to determine how well the students do, to make sure they've completed their work, to make sure they're focused. All the responsibility is actually on them.

An important note: choice and responsibility are related but distinct. You could give students choice (choose your topic, choose your method of study) without giving them responsibility (it's up to you to ensure that you get a good education). We were getting neither.

I started to think about this all the time during my junior year. Because when I realized that, from the ages of fourteen to eighteen, teenagers have almost no real responsibility in school, I was genuinely shocked. How can we expect kids to emerge from high school as responsible adults if they never experience real responsibility in school?

What's more, isn't one of the key goals of an education system to prepare the next generation to inherit the earth? Isn't the goal to cultivate stewards so that, in the future, the planet and society are in better hands than they were in the previous generation? But how can high school cultivate stewards if it never lets them practice stewardship? For four years, I realized, we steward high schoolers, like a flock of sheep, when we should be slowly handing them the reins.

It was this deep, pervasive, insidious flaw of high school that I wanted to fix first in my new school. Because it made no sense to me, none whatsoever, that high schoolers didn't have any ownership over their own education.

Once Sam began muttering about how enfeebled he and his friends were at school, I started to notice how true this was. Until then, when I'd drop by his school to attend a meeting or bring him his baseball uniform, I tended to notice whether kids were smiling or frowning, whether they seemed lonely or were having fun with friends. Now, whether I bumped into the cheery superstar or the sulky kid who was failing, all I could see was that most of the students seemed to be following someone else's script. Looking at the way they walked down the halls and sat in their classrooms, listening to them talk about their work, I realized that not one of them felt this was *their* education. Looking closely at their faces, I began to realize Sam was right—this couldn't be the best way for them to move forward.

When I asked James—this was a few weeks after the day on the fire escape—what he felt was missing from school, his answer surprised me. "I wish we could go more in depth, sometimes." At first blush, this seemed odd. He's a smart guy, but he struggled in high school. He got terrible grades in math and science, and his results elsewhere were unpredictable. He'd ace a history paper one week and get an F the next week. He battled with his teachers, and some of them hated him—thought he was insolent and rude. He and Red caused endless trouble when they were placed in classes together, and I wasn't always removed from this. Our freshman year James and I got booted out of our English class for playing pranks.

James wasn't considered a good student. So, at first, I expected him to say he wished we could have more free time or do sports during the day or watch films. And yet, when I reflected a little more carefully, I wasn't so surprised. Outside of school, James often became obsessed with specific pursuits, and these obsessions would take over his life for months at a time. He decided he wanted to be a filmmaker, and every weekend for six months we would spend all of Friday afternoon, Saturday, and Sunday morning making a film that he had dreamed up.

Then he wanted to be a cop. He went to a state trooper academy in the summer. He interned for six months at the police station in town. He got a crew cut and started wearing his shirt tucked into his navy blue shorts. Then he discovered snowboarding. He started wearing baggy snow pants, giant sweatshirts, and bandannas. He'd come to school every Monday limping and wincing because he had tried some new trick that was out of his depth. Then there was fashion, then hiking, then karate, then boxing.

His teachers thought these were just phases, passing fancies, a sign of his lack of seriousness. But what was really happening was that he was searching for exactly the thing he told me he wanted: more depth. He wanted to dive into something, to really grapple with it, to become an expert in it, and since he wasn't getting that at school, he searched for it elsewhere, often finding things that didn't quite meet his intense desire to become a master at something.

He got it, eventually. He was accepted into a small middle-tier college that most people haven't heard of to study sports management.

But he found that the other students weren't curious, weren't interested, weren't passionate. So a fun-loving goofball who had spent a lot of high school partying buckled down and became a bookworm. He quickly rose to the top of his class and joined the dean's list. By the end of that year, he was able to apply and transfer to Syracuse University. And again, he quickly moved to the top. Along the way, he found a fancy that was more than a fancy. He's now as knowledgeable on conflicts in the Middle East and the EU as anyone I've met, and he's been offered a prestigious place at LSE to study them.

It didn't take me long to suspect that James wasn't alone in pining for the chance to experience real mastery. Soon I saw it as another shocking hole in the American high school experience. It wasn't that we didn't get *enough* mastery or experience *enough* depth in school. It was lacking altogether. The closest we ever came were book reports and extended projects, which, compared to really taking ownership of a discipline, a topic, an endeavor, were like drops in the ocean. This is the difference between reading a summary of Einstein's theories in a textbook and re-deriving his equations for the theory of relativity; the difference between reading *Auto Repair for Dummies* and building an engine from the ground up.

Again, this befuddled me. Weren't we expected to master something eventually? Get a job, a career, make a difference in the world? Wasn't that part of being an adult? How could we get there if we never got to practice mastery in high school? Expertise, it seemed to me, was like anything else. It required practice. Yet we were being flung into the game of life without so much as a scrimmage.

I saw all of this a little differently from Sam. To me, it wasn't just that his friends were prevented from learning how to master things, though this was true. But just as bad, the absence of true mastery meant the absence of true engagement. Years before he undertook the beeper study, Csikszentmihalyi had identified a new psychological phenomenon: flow. He had shown that under certain circumstances people could become so immersed in what they were doing that they lost any awareness of what was going on around them, how much time was passing, or who else was near them. Anyone who plays a musical instrument, tinkers with machines, or writes knows what he was talking about. Further, he argued, the chance to feel such flow frequently was essential to well-being.

When he and Larson began studying teenagers, they noted that the kids who regularly experienced such flow were the ones who seemed to thrive and do well as they got older. These episodes of flow, which he and Larson renamed "negentropy" (the opposite of the decay and decline entailed in "entropy"), seemed to buffer kids against the unavoidable frustrations and lows of adolescent life. When did the teenagers in the study feel such engagement, focus, and absorption? When they were hot in the pursuit of mastery—it could be music, mathematics, theater, or politics. The researchers discovered, however, that such negentropy was the exception, not the rule. Few of the kids in the study spent significant time immersed in something they cared deeply about. This meant that, for the most part, kids had few chances to learn *how to* master things and rarely experienced the fulfillment and happiness the pursuit of mastery could bring them.

Considering a student's typical day at school, it is no wonder this is true. How could a fifteen-year-old become really good at something if he was required to switch activities every forty-two minutes? How could a seventeen-year-old face the challenge of excellence if she rarely had the chance to toil away night and day at something she really cared about? The school day, and the kind of work it offered, was one big, fat barrier to the intensity and drive teenagers most need.

Not long before Sam tripped over this problem of mastery, Angela Duckworth, a psychologist at the University of Pennsylvania, published an exciting new study showing that self-discipline, rather than intelligence, was the best predictor of success in high school. Her work revived an important old idea—that effort was more valuable than intrinsic ability. She followed this study with an intriguing new construct: grit, a combination of self-discipline, interest, perseverance, and purpose. Duckworth set out to show that if we could instill grit in our students, we'd go a long way toward improving the educational prospects of underachievers. Think of the kid who decides she'll do anything to become a first-rate debater, volleyball player, or science student. She spends every spare minute practicing, learning, devoting herself to her goal.

On the face of it, Duckworth's grit was not that different from Sam's mastery—except for one thing. Most of the psychologists and educators who liked the idea of grit became hell-bent on figuring out how to teach kids self-control. In other words, instead of making room in school for kids to find things that would elicit grittiness, they felt sure they could simply train kids to try harder, concentrate more, delay gratification, and keep their eyes on the prize. However, so far, there is little evidence that you can train kids to be more self-disciplined for tasks they don't care about.

As my kids made their way through high school, I noticed teachers trying to encourage or admonish kids to finish their homework, stop glancing at their friend in the next seat, and concentrate on the lesson. But neither Sam nor I saw much attention given to the kind of desire or single-minded purpose that might spur kids to grittiness.

When I first set out, in the beginning of my junior year, my visions of a new school were still mired in traditional approaches. After all, I had been part of traditional school my whole life. As a result, in the beginning, I thought we could keep the traditional subjects intact: science, the humanities, math, English, foreign languages, and so on. The difference would be that students would have more control over what they studied within those subjects. In biology "class," rather than being told exactly what parts of the cell to study, kids could choose to study lions or mitochondria or vernal pools. Whatever they wanted, as long as it was biology!

It wasn't until the summer before my senior year, the summer before the Independent Project began, that I suddenly realized this conception was both dated and flawed.

What dawned on me that summer was that studying subjects just didn't make sense anymore. Maybe in the Victorian era, when it was important for a well-respected gentleman to be moderately well versed in many different subjects—but not in the twenty-first century. I can list about a thousand reasons why not, but there were a few big ones that struck me that summer. We live in the age of the Internet, when information is literally at people's fingertips, all the time. Having lots of information stored in your head, on its own, is not very useful. That's what Google is for! This may sound glib, but I don't mean it to be. I'm not saying information isn't valuable—not at all—but memorizing it is a waste of time in our information-saturated society. Instead, we have a deluge of information, and learning how to sift through it, becoming curious about it, learning how to discern between reliable and unreliable information, how to absorb and articulate it—that's how we should be spending our time.

Second, to the degree that being well-rounded is important, learning bits of history and science and math doesn't actually lead to well-roundedness, partly because when knowledge is discretized the way it is in school, people start to think of themselves as science people or humanities people, which doesn't help much with well-roundedness, but also because knowing a little bit of biology doesn't help you understand an article in a newspaper about new research that's come out. Having a bit of mathematical knowledge doesn't help you understand the role that mathematicians played in developing the military's new weapon. Instead, to become well-rounded academically, you need to learn to think like a scientist or a mathematician or a historian. Only then can you become well-rounded in a meaningful sense. Only then can you use those disciplines to understand new information, to make more informed voting decisions, to appreciate the world in more varied ways, to be a better employee, and ultimately to get more enjoyment out of life.

And finally, the real world isn't broken down into categories. I've been out of high school for only a few years now, but the problems I've faced—whether starting a garden, organizing a ball, or conducting evolutionary biology experiments—all lie at the intersection of different subjects. The real world almost always requires an interdisciplinary approach.

I knew just what Sam meant. My own sense of the mismatch between the curriculum and the world came, in part, from my experience working in liberal arts colleges. Where I teach, at Williams College, professors talk constantly about the balance between offering students specific expertise in a field (in my case psychology, but it could be English literature, quantum physics, or American history) and providing them with a set of intellectual skills that are essential regardless of their major. Now, in 2016 many of us still want students to learn what Charles Eliot, president of Harvard University from 1869 to 1909, wanted them to learn a century ago: the ability to think carefully about a new idea, the ability to draw on data to form an opinion, the ability to use what they know to learn something they don't know—in short, the ability to think well.

Strangely, there are few clear expositions of what good thinking entails—at least expositions that would be useful to educators. Most schools (including colleges) assume that they are teaching their students to think well, without articulating what good thinking really is, or what it takes to learn to do it. This disjuncture is particularly striking (and egregious) in high school. A lot of what students between the ages of fourteen and eighteen spend their school time on has little to do with building ideas, developing opinions, asking questions, or finding answers. Follow a tenth grader around for a day and this becomes vividly clear.

I watched Serena, a sophomore, from 8 a.m. until 2:20, when her school day ended. Here's how it went: she spent twenty minutes in homeroom chatting idly with her best friend. She didn't like her homeroom teacher, so she didn't talk to him at all. Then the bell rang and she rushed to English, a course pitched to the middle-ability kids who had no learning problems, weren't on the vocational track, but weren't headed for AP courses either. Once in the room, Serena spent the first five minutes getting settled and saying hello to a friend; the next

twelve minutes correcting mistakes, along with the class, on a vocabulary homework sheet; and fifteen minutes summarizing a chapter of a
novel, *All Quiet on the Western Front* (the only novel they read all year).
Out of twenty-three students, five contributed to this summary (with
some additions from the teacher). Then they spent ten minutes discussing whether they could identify with Paul, the protagonist, and one
minute going over the homework, and then it was time to go to the
next class. I followed her through six more classes (math, art, American
history, Spanish, gym, and computer) and I saw some version of the
same thing in each class. If a cognitive psychologist had charted the moments in the day calling for higher-order thinking, she might have found
enough to fill eight minutes. Except perhaps halfway through lunch
when Serena and her friends got into an argument about whether
Mexican families should be allowed across the border. That was the
closest thing to a serious discussion I saw. It's fair to say that, though
good thinking is the cornerstone of a good education and one of the
few things we can agree all adults need, we spend precious little time
on it in high school.

Sadly, there is solid evidence that high school is indeed failing to
have a substantive impact on how students reason. Recently, Andrew
Shtulman, a psychologist at Occidental College, asked high school and
college students to explain their reasons for believing in a variety of invisible entities (ghosts, god, and fairies, for example). Students who had
not only graduated from high school but gained admission to selective
colleges were no more sophisticated in the reasons they offered for
their beliefs than high school students. Given the fact that using evidence to back up a belief or opinion is one of the prime components of
higher-order thinking, Shtulman's data suggest that kids are graduating
from high school no more sophisticated in their ability to reason than
they were when they began. In my own lab we have data supporting
this. Asked to convince others of their position on a controversial topic,
students at the best colleges in the country have difficulty backing up
their arguments with evidence. How did we come to have a high school
curriculum that did not teach the most important skill: good thinking?

A confluence of historical events got us here. During the early nine-teenth century, as educators tried to teach more and more students to think in complex and abstract ways, they came up with the reasonable idea that if they broke these processes down into their components, they could teach more children more efficiently. Meanwhile, psychol-ogy, a burgeoning new field, appeared to be teasing apart the strands that went into reasoning, problem solving, and decision making. Some-how, once researchers had identified the components of higher-order thinking, it seemed to make sense to teach those components sepa-rately. But if you never are asked to think about complex things that actually matter to you, practicing the parts of good thinking does not lead anywhere.

More recently, a wide range of seemingly unrelated studies have pro-vided evidence for something my own mother would tell me is obvious, but apparently is not. The best way to develop inquiry is to have lots of opportunities to become curious about things and to pursue that curiosity. The best way to learn how to take apart someone else's ar-gument is for students to get into lots of discussions about interesting controversial topics, with enough guidance so that they are nudged to exchange views in a reasoned and open-minded way. Finally, the best way to get students to think about the scientific method is to ask them to critique the work of other scientists. However, what students actu-ally do, day in and day out, in the class and in their homework is quite different from this. For four years they are asked to work at a whole host of specific and somewhat isolated tasks, studying all kinds of topics (learning formulas for geometry, memorizing species' names, following instructions, expanding vocabularies, writing five-paragraph essays). It seems as if we hope that when students come out the other side, at graduation, all those rituals and sheets of paper will have somehow magically transformed them into better thinkers.

Watching Sam mull over his new school and figure out what the students would do each day, I began to realize that we had all been tinkering—longer periods, more hands-on activities, kids working on

certain projects in groups, longer lunch, shorter lunch, Spanish requirement, creative project during May, more tests, fewer tests. All
reasonable changes, but none that really get at the fundamental problem. Imagine you owned a restaurant, and each week fewer and fewer
people came because they didn't like the food. You could change the
curtains, hire a friendlier waiter, play music in the background, or even
offer $5 off the main course. Any one of those things might improve
the restaurant a little bit, might temporarily distract your customers
from the unsatisfying meals. But in the end, a mediocre meal doesn't
taste different because of new curtains. The only real solution would
be to make better food. Similarly, if students are supposed to get better at thinking while in high school, but spend almost no time engaged
in any real thinking, chances are that no matter how long the periods
are, how often they take field trips, or how challenging the vocabulary
worksheets, they're not going to get better at thinking.

There was a lot of emphasis in my school on family, teamwork, and
collaboration. People used to say that when the high schools in the
local area were characterized, ours was described as "one big hug."
My freshman year of high school I played shortstop and pitcher for
the JV baseball team, and in my senior year I co-captained the varsity
basketball team. For all three coaches, teamwork was the main thing
emphasized. "That's how Falcons excel," they used to say. "By being
the best teammates on the court."

And yet, I noticed, this ethic was entirely absent from the classroom. In school, collaboration is usually thought of as cheating. On
the rare occasion when we did work together in school, for example, on
a "group" project, it was largely superficial. The project, which might
be to create a science poster or make a presentation together, was collaborative only because the teacher said so. These projects could have
easily been accomplished by one person. Students had to artificially
divide up the labor to make it a "group" endeavor.

In the real world, as far as I could tell, collaboration was often necessary. Project Sprout had made this abundantly clear to me. It would

have been physically impossible for me to cultivate a two-acre plot and organize pig roast fund-raisers for five hundred people on my own.

Once again, it seemed wild to me that we never got to practice true collaboration in school. Time and again, it seemed, there was a skill with which we were expected to leave high school that we never really practiced while we were there. On top of that, I knew from the baseball diamond and the basketball court and the farm and the garden that collaboration felt incredible. If it was something we needed to learn, and something that was rewarding to do, why the hell was it missing entirely from the school day?

I could've answered Sam's emphatic question. When teens are together, sparks fly. The psychological literature on adolescent development is stuffed with articles showing how important peers are to teens. They feel dull, flat, and misunderstood when they are separated from their friends, and the opposite when they are together. In fact, when a group of teenagers who like each other gather, little else seems quite as important to them. Certainly not a teacher or a textbook. Or that's the conventional wisdom, and the explanation for keeping them apart. How will they get their work done if they are flirting, fighting, plotting, and commiserating?

And yet, a whole host of studies has shown that when students work together, they learn more. But it's not just that collaborating doesn't get in the way of learning. It is an essential skill in and of itself. In schools where kids are encouraged to help one another and solve problems together, bullying decreases, academic skills improve, and the overall climate of the school becomes more positive. Nor is this just a matter of encouraging friendships or discouraging meanness. It's a matter of doing good work. If you could accomplish things only when you didn't help anyone or get help, if you could work only when no one spoke to you, if you could do a good job only when you weren't required to compromise, where would you be as an adult? If you think about it this way, as Sam began to while designing his school, it becomes clear that the enormous energy teachers expend keeping kids apart while they learn is the opposite of what they need. They are asked to learn separately, when in fact what they need is a chance to become good at learning together.

There's a single statue in front of my high school. It's a giant hunk of oxidized metal, and it's the first thing you see when you drive up. It's meant to stand out because it's supposed to represent what our school stands for. Carved into the face of the metal is the inscription "How will I make my mark on the world?"

"Cool," I used to think. Cool that I go to a school where that's what matters. Not how will I excel, or how will I be happy, but how will I make my mark on the world, how will I make the world a better place? That's what we care about here at Green River.

But was it? All throughout my junior year, I felt my eyes opening a little wider every day. In thinking about how to make school better, in designing my new school, I began to see things that hadn't stood out before. Did we really emphasize having an impact on the world? Did we have any real engagement with the outside world at all?

The truth is, I started to notice, with the exception of Friday night basketball games, school was pretty isolated from the outside community. I had always assumed that one of the goals of education, particularly high school, was to engage you with the world, to make you care for it, and to teach you how to become a better steward of it. This, to me, was one of the ways education made the world a better place: by making people better citizens. It's certainly what we said we were all about at Green River.

And yet, when in our classrooms did we do anything that really contributed to our community, locally or globally? We learned about the world and occasionally (though perhaps rarely) about our local community. But did we try to contribute to it? Did we try to reduce hunger or make our school greener? Did we contribute to the proposals to redesign Main Street? Did we write letters to the editor about political issues? Did we clean up the river?

None of that. Not in the classroom. In fact, we never practiced any kind of meaningful stewardship at all. We were never asked to solve any real problems in the real world. And once again, I found myself wondering how we could be expected to learn to care for the world, to want to dedicate our lives to making it better, to become thoughtful, contributing citizens if we never practiced any of that in school.

Good question. And Sam wasn't the first to worry about it. In his classic book on human development *Childhood and Society*, Erik Erikson argued that the mighty battle of adolescence involves finding one's place in the world. It isn't enough for a teenager to have a loving relationship with parents or do well at school or make good friends, though these are important. The real crisis of adolescence, Erikson argued, is figuring out how to fit into the larger community—what work you'll do, what role you'll play, what impact you'll have. In adolescence children feel the first stirrings of responsibility. They yearn to have an impact on the adult world they are entering. This often unfolds hand in hand with their intense interest in right and wrong, their hunger for justice. One need only think of Vietnam War protests, Occupy Wall Street, or the climate change movement to see how powerful social concerns are during the teenage years. And yet, high schools tend to push activism to the sidelines, if they allow it at all.

Schools, however inadvertently, go to great efforts to circumvent the teenage craving to be part of society. By keeping them all day in buildings where they are only with other people their age, or professionals trained to interact with them, we isolate them from the world they yearn to enter. By discouraging their activism, as so many schools do, we keep a lid on the very engagement they crave and need.

These were the major problems I saw in the current system: lack of autonomy, lack of engagement, lack of mastery, learning information rather than habits of mind, lack of serious thinking, lack of true collaboration, and lack of interaction with the outside world.

Some of the solutions to these problems seemed simple and came to me immediately, and others took months of deliberation.

How to increase autonomy was plain: just give students more autonomy. Make them the authors of their own education. Let high schoolers be in charge of high school. Given my experience with the garden, I had a hunch that if students were in charge, this would take care of the engagement problem, too. If you choose what you learn, you're likely to want to learn it.

Equally, how to increase the experience of mastery in high school was as easy as pie. Give students a chance to master something. In fact, in my new school, they'd have half the day to focus on mastering a single thing. For the whole school year, if necessary. Why half a day? It couldn't be the whole day, because there were other things, like academics, that we needed to do. Anything less than half didn't seem like enough time to really delve into something, to really become an expert. I'd call this something an Individual Endeavor. It could be anything—build a boat, write a play, conduct an experiment—as long as it was involved enough to take up your time and you were excited to do it.

Figuring out how to approach academics was a little trickier. I had decided that subjects were totally last year's news. Or last century's news. So that part was easy. I would scrap the subjects in their traditional form. Rather than learn math or English, we would learn how to think like mathematicians or work like writers. Instead of focusing on what specific knowledge we would learn, the school would focus on making students better thinkers.

But that didn't solve the whole problem, not on its own. Because I would still be too late. We had all already gone through so many years of education in "subjects" that the students in my new school might already think of themselves as "math people" or "arts people." Even though I was fascinated by psychology and loved to write fiction I, too, had somehow started thinking of myself as a math-and-science person, not an arts-and-humanities person. Many of my friends already had serious math phobias, so getting them to think like mathematicians was a daunting task.

This second aspect of the problem plagued me all summer long.

I spent hours mulling over how to break the curse of academic typecasting.

We could have two weeks in the beginning of the year where students who thought of themselves as science people could study only the humanities, and vice versa. But that seemed forced and artificial, and suffered from the same ills that I was trying to cure. Forcing students to do science wasn't the way to make them love it.

So, instead, we could bring in scientists, historians, mathematicians, and artists and have them each give a talk on why everyone should be interested in their discipline. But again, I already knew how much high schoolers loved to rebel against things. As soon as some adult came in and told us we *should* like art, we'd decide we *wouldn't*. I came up with endless gimmicks, tricks, approaches, and methods to solve the problem, but none of them rang true.

Finally, I realized I needed to go back to square one. I had gotten so caught up in clever solutions, I had stopped thinking about the problem: that, somehow, in our educational society, math was linked to science and humanities were coupled with the arts and you identified with either one pair or the other. And that was the problem, wasn't it? Those groupings were meaningless.

The idea was simple: I would rejigger the traditional groupings of the subjects. I realized that the disciplines of science and humanities have a lot more in common with each other than science does with math or the humanities with English, despite the classic pairings. Similarly, math and English have a lot more in common with each other than either does with science or history!

To work in the humanities and the physical sciences, you need to think like a scientist. You need to learn the art of asking a question and how to use the scientific method to find an answer to that question. To work in English and math, you need to learn how to think and communicate in a language. In the case of English, that language is, well, English, and you need to learn how to read it and write it. In math, that language is the language of mathematics, and you need to learn how to think in mathematical terms and express things in the language of numbers and logic. You use English to describe the world, and you do the same with math.

So in my new school we would have two disciplines: the sciences and the languages. Mixing up the pairings of the standard disciplines would, I hoped, prevent the usual subject prejudices and would allow us to learn new habits of mind, not just information within each subject.

The question, then, was how to actually go about learning the sciences and the languages. Well, it seemed clear that our method should spring directly from the nature of the disciplines. The sciences are about asking questions. So for the period of time when we were focusing on the sciences, the students would work on the art of asking and answering questions. They would start each week coming up with their own natural and social science questions. The other students, and any available teachers with expertise in the sciences, would critique the question and help make it a better question, thereby helping all of us to improve on the art of asking a good question. Then the students would spend the week answering their questions—doing research and experiments, reading, and talking to experts (both inside and outside the school), and on Friday they would teach their answers to the group. Again, the other students and teachers would give critical feedback on the way the students went about getting their answers, the quality of the answers they presented, and how well they taught their answers to the group.

In the same vein, I proceeded under the conviction that languages are something you learn by practicing (by practicing I don't mean drilling; I mean doing). So for the literary language, we would practice the art of reading and writing. Each week one student would choose a novel for the group to read, and at the end of the week each person would read from a piece of writing he or she did in response to the novel. For the mathematical language, we would practice logical and mathematical reasoning, with each student choosing a topic or challenge to tackle.

So the problem of academics was solved. What about the problem of collaboration? Again, this was something I struggled with for months. It was very slippery for me, because the key was that the collaboration had to be genuine and necessary, not an artifice. So how would I make collaboration a required element of the school, but keep it organic and real?

The answer came, as it so often does, unexpectedly. One night, maybe three-quarters of the way through my junior year, my mom told me about something she was trying out in an experimental school she had helped start. The idea was that young children could get their whole "curriculum" through collaborative enterprises. At the beginning of the year, the kids would pick a venture to work on together, and then they would spend the year creating and executing it. And here was the kicker: the endeavor had to be something that actually helped others in a real way.

For example, one group of children, ages six to eleven, decided to run the school apothecary. Through this process, they would learn about botany and medicine and ecology. They would learn about financing, bookkeeping, and economics. But they would also learn about helping people, about being responsible for something, about building something from the ground up, about creating a real product. And all of it would occur in a natural, real, and exciting way.

I knew immediately that this had to be a part of the Independent Project. It could solve not only the problem of collaboration but that of engagement with the outside world as well. At the very end of the school year, the group would come together and decide on a Collective Endeavor, the only requirement being that whatever they decided to do would solve a real problem in their community, either locally or globally: improve homeless shelters, clean up the water table, make the school carbon neutral—anything.

The basic structure of my new school had taken shape: half a day for an Individual Endeavor, half a day for academics; half of our academic time devoted to the sciences, asking and answering questions, and half of our academic time devoted to the mathematical and literary languages. Then, at the end of the school year, everything else would stop and the students would team up for a Collective Endeavor. And that was it: the whole "curriculum."

Because the students would be in charge, they would be engaged, they'd discover real responsibility, and they'd be empowered by their newfound ownership of their school. Through the Individual Endeavor, kids would discover and practice mastery. They would also get to work on something that truly excited them and, whatever their endeavor was, they would learn a variety of skills through it. In the academics, students would improve various habits of mind that weren't focused on traditionally. They would learn to think and work like scientists, mathematicians, writers, historians, and in a way that granted them autonomy, making them more likely to digest and embody the approaches they studied.

When I look at our educational system, I often think of the many horrible roadways I have traveled over the years. For instance, if you drive from Westchester County, New York, to Middletown, Connecticut, as I have, on occasion, you have to navigate a bewildering, senseless, and circuitous maze of raised highways, parallel roads, and unnecessary detours. As I make my way through all the hideous and confusing routes, it seems clear how those cement jungles occurred. As populations grew and car travel expanded, old roads no longer sufficed. So states added a highway here, an overpass there, a second expressway, another route to a bridge—in short, a series of fixes built on a system that really didn't fit the new era. In the same way, our high schools have added, subtracted, extended bit by bit, to accommodate new educational goals and changing school populations. Often the system incorporates some particular practice based on the politics of the day, or one new finding from research. In many ways the overall approach, like those bad highways, makes no sense, though each piece seemed to at a given time. Such piecemeal change is forgivable with roads. You can't easily dismantle highways and begin from scratch.

But you can in a school. This was what I saw Sam doing as he envisioned his new school. His tremendous frustration and his innate sense of optimism had led him to question the whole setup. And as so often happens, that sense of a new beginning had led him to a set of fresh and vibrant ideas about how to make a school that really worked for teenagers.

There was only one last thing my new school needed: a name. Fortunately, it came to me fully formed, all at once. I knew it was right. But it's funny. In the years since, all the talks I've given, all the conversations I've had, the e-mails I've received, no one's ever once asked me why I called it the Independent Project.

I named it that for a few reasons. First, I like names that have the word "project" in them. I had coined the name for Project Sprout, three years before. "Project" gave it a sense of moving forward—like it was a mission. And even before I had a name, when I started telling teachers about my idea for a new school, they said, "But we already have that! You can just do an independent study!" I loved that they so didn't get it, that they didn't see the difference between my vision for a new school and forty minutes a day set aside for research on a topic of choice. "Independent study" captured so much of what was wrong with traditional school that it just had to be part of the name of my new school. And sure enough, the name caused a lot of confusion. For months, people referred to it as the Independent *Study*, or the *Independence* Project, or *an* Independent Project. "The Independent Project" was such a simple name, and yet so slippery for people, and the mistakes they made in calling it by name were subtle yet profound.

By the time you've finished step two, you will have thought openly and thoroughly about the purpose of high school and identified the essential ingredients of a good education. Your list may not be exactly like the list another group in another community would come up with. But it should reflect what scientists have learned about adolescence, education, and learning—it should be based on some evidence. And it should address the needs and wants of other students in your school.

Then, putting aside questions about logistics and ignoring obstacles, you will have figured out what you would change about school to make it fit your ideas. These ideas might involve the daily schedule, what students will do each day, or how people will interact.

It's essential here not to get bogged down by thinking about what's realistic or what will be acceptable to others. Envision your ideal school. But don't stop there. It's not enough to espouse lofty goals: "kids should love books" or "students will become good citizens." You need to buckle down and do the hard work of fleshing out what it takes to make those things happen. The concrete details matter.

3

BUILD IT

A dream design is only that: a dream. In order for it to matter, it has to become a reality. For that to happen you need to go through the slow, laborious, and at times painful process of actually building a new school.

Up until now, your new school exists only in your head, and maybe in the heads of a few others you've talked to about it. Now it becomes a real, physical thing. This is a turning point. It can be really fun, and it can be really hard.

You might actually be laying down mortar and brick. You might be applying for a charter or raising money. You might be inviting people around to your house in the evenings. Or, if you're like Sam, you are trying to convince a suite of public school officials and staff to formally approve your project.

In the design stage you were supposed to be limitless. Now the limits become essential. Your dream gets molded by the obstacles and challenges in your way. Part of this process is adjusting your design to fit the constraints of reality, and part of this process is doing whatever you can to overcome those obstacles. In other words, this is the nitty-gritty—where compromises, letdowns, agreements, and triumphs come into play.

This chapter is about building your new school. For Sam, this involved three stages. First, getting the Independent Project approved as a school within a school in his public high school in western Massachusetts. Second, deciding which students would actually partake in the school. And third, building (or finding) the physical space that the school would occupy.

At the end of this chapter, your feet will be firmly planted in the office of a girls' locker room. Sorry to give away the ending, but there is no real suspense in this part of the story anyway. I built a new school.

But I'm often perplexed, looking back, by the path the Independent Project took to fruition. In going through the events of the year that led up to the Independent Project—my junior year of high school—I'm struck, first and foremost, by the vehement resistance I experienced. I wasn't surprised then, and I'm still not now, by the resistance itself. Any change worth making meets obstacles. But as I recall the hurdles we leapt that year, I find the severity of some of the responses to my idea startling. At the time, I took it all in stride—I didn't know what to expect, so I had no expectations. It's only now, through the lens of distance and perspective, that I find the image of a middle-aged teacher shouting at a sixteen-year-old that "kids cannot be trusted to learn on their own" both hilarious and troubling. Back then, it was just par for the course.

That course began with Mr. Huron, shortly after the first conversation with my mom at the dinner table. It must have been early October of my junior year. I had decided I was going to start a school; now I just needed to make it happen. I knew I needed to *design* the school too—its curriculum, its structure, its components. But I also knew that changing something in a school takes a long time. When I wanted to start Project Sprout, I had to spend months trying to get it approved. And that was just a garden! This was a new school. Getting it approved could take *forever*. So I wasn't going to wait until my design was complete to begin building the school. I had to start right away.

And I started right away by going to see Mr. Huron. I needed an adult on board. I wasn't stupid—I understood that creating a new school would ruffle feathers. So I needed someone who had knowledge about the process for getting something like this approved, someone who was close to the other teachers, who could talk to them, influence them. I also knew that adults don't like to listen to kids. I needed a grown-up to fight in my corner, so that other grown-ups would take my idea seriously.

Mr. Huron and I had worked on Project Sprout together. We had toiled side by side almost every day of high school and, along the way, had grown incredibly close. By the end of high school, not only did we run the garden together; he was also my basketball coach, the faculty adviser to the Independent Project, and one of my best friends. We hiked together, played tennis together, and went to conferences together. He even took care of me one night when I had food poisoning.

But even if I had hated him, Mr. Huron would have been the right person to go to. First, he believed strongly in the power of youth, and in the wonderful things that can happen when you hand young people the reins. He had both witnessed and been a part of making that happen in the garden, with tremendous results. Second, he was a master of being invisible. He was the kind of guy who led from behind, staying in the background, letting students stand out front. If there was a newspaper article about Project Sprout, he refused to be mentioned in it. At board meetings, he leaned way back in his chair, so that you almost forgot he was there, and kept quiet. If he spoke, it was only at the very end, once everyone else had talked, and only then to make subtle suggestions, never commands or orders. It was an adult like this—one who truly believed that young people are powerful, one who trusted them in a deep, serious way, one who could be invisible, and one who could lead without being a leader—that would be essential for this school to be truly different from anything that came before it.

There was one other reason Mr. Huron was the right adult to work with on my new school: it was the way he responded when I first told him my idea. I walked into his open office, without an appointment (something that perpetually infuriated his assistant but which he never mentioned). He got up and closed the door behind me, which always made me feel like what I had to say was important. I sat down, and I said, "I want to start a school within a school at Green River. I want it to be student run." Almost everyone else I would tell this to in the coming weeks and months would laugh, or ask if I was serious, or start pointing out reasons it wouldn't work. But Mr. Huron looked me straight in the eye, and for a little while he said nothing. And then he said, "Okay. What do you need from me to make it happen?"

* * *

Mr. Huron was nothing like the guidance counselors I had encountered in the many schools I had observed or the ones I had read about in books on education. He spent hardly any time in his office. It was just a place to leave his jacket and pile up papers he wished he could avoid. He seemed fairly uninterested in filling out forms, putting together college application packets, or even meeting with parents and social workers. He definitely wasn't a desk guy. Instead, every time I went into the school building, morning, afternoon, or after school, he was walking in his bouncy, athletic way toward some activity with kids: a sports practice, the garden, a group protesting fossil fuels, or hiking a nearby mountain with tenth and eleventh graders. It wasn't just that he loved teenagers, though that came through loud and clear. It was that, to him, the best way, the only way, to guide students was to do things with them—hike, meet, play tennis, or weed a garden. When he said to Sam, "What do you need from me?" his words captured the quality that made him such an extraordinary presence in the school— he thought of himself as a support and a resource for the things kids wanted to do, rather than as a therapist, a disciplinarian, or a bureaucrat. Nor was it just that he reached out to kids, eager to help with whatever grabbed them most. He embodied another crucial quality— the urge to connect.

When I first met Mr. Huron, he seemed like the quintessential small-town guy—upstanding, polite, slightly awkward with middle-aged women like me, more comfortable on a playing field than in a meeting. He grew up in the community and was a star soccer and basketball player in high school. Now, in his thirties, he had a short buzz cut and the posture of someone in the military. He drove a pickup, was married to his high school sweetheart, and coached youth sports in his spare time. But under all of that lay something quite different, something vital to good guidance counseling and therefore to a good education. As I would come to find out, watching him with my three sons and countless other kids, Mr. Huron had a nearly bottomless appetite for getting to know people, especially young people, and for forging relationships.

Whether he would say it this way himself or not, he seemed to know that you can't guide teenagers unless you really know them. And you can't really know them if they don't also know you. In other words, at the heart of any good high school counseling lies an authentic relationship between adult and teen.

Sam saw Mr. Huron as a crucial advocate and source of support while he navigated the tangled vines of adult skepticism and high school bureaucracy, but I saw something different. I saw someone who really got teenagers. He had taken one of the most underrated and sidelined roles in secondary education, that of guidance counselor, and put it at the center of the educational experience.

The conventional wisdom about mentoring is that kids from poor backgrounds or troubled families are the ones who need a mentor, a "big brother," or a caring teacher. But this represents a misunderstanding of the role of mentors in the development of all teenagers, rich or poor, stable or troubled. As children loosen ties with their parents, they look out into the world for influences and emotional bonds. This process helps them become part of the *world*, rather than simply part of their *family*.

For that process to work well, a couple of elements are necessary. Each student has to feel a real emotional bond with an adult in school. Forty-five minutes in a class with a teacher at the front, no matter how skilled, dynamic, or smart that teacher may be, won't cut it. Students need to spend sustained time with that adult (this may be why coaches often seem to have such a connection to their players). And though time is necessary, it's not sufficient. Young people need to work alongside such adults, sharing aspirations, personal experiences, fun, disappointment, and confidences. And the interactions need to unfold in the context of pursuits that matter to those particular students. This is why the fifteen-minute community meeting that so many schools have adopted as a way of starting the day does not work. Adults and teens need to make things together, argue and solve logistical problems, talk about people and places, share successes and failures. I saw Mr. Huron do all of this with Sam and his friends.

I don't think Sam and Mr. Huron realized what they had stumbled upon as they began to hatch their plans for the new school. By forming something that was part friendship, part collaboration, and just a tiny part guidance counselor and student, they had taken a crucial first step in establishing the new school. Sam's steam fueled this particular engine. But Mr. Huron's readiness to help a student implement his plan was essential. During the ensuing year, Sam and I each realized, I think, that the impact of his school rested on the fact that it was run by students. But equally important, we both saw that it demanded a new, more potent role for adults. Mr. Huron was the IP's first adult.

In conversations that mirrored the ones that were happening at the dinner table, Mr. Huron and I began talking about the Independent Project every day. We mulled over what it would look like, how the day would be structured, what we would study, and especially how to make it happen. And Mr. H said that the very first thing we needed to do was get the superintendent and principal on board.

In any story about a high schooler trying to start a new school, different adults will play the roles of heroes and villains. In someone else's story, the guidance counselor might play the antagonist, hell-bent on stopping the school from happening. In mine, of course, he was one of the heroes. Similarly, the head honchos of the school—the principal and superintendent—could easily fill the role of power-hungry tyrants, old-fashioned, rigid squares, or cheery, bureaucratic, spineless antivillains. In my story, the principal and superintendent weren't exactly heroes, but they weren't villains, either. They were supportive supporting cast.

Both the principal and superintendent were, from the get-go, open to the idea of the Independent Project. Often, when I get e-mails from students in northern Idaho or Western Australia who want to start something like the Independent Project at their schools, one of the first questions is: how did you get the principal on board? And as soon as I start to tell them that I was fortunate in this regard, that my principal was open-minded, they throw up their hands and say, "Well, see, there you have it; won't happen in a million years at my school." Yes, I was very lucky to have supportive members of the administration. But if we hadn't had such open-minded leaders, the first step wouldn't have been to seek their support. Instead, we would have rallied all the faculty first, and then used them to sway the administration. There will always be heroes and villains: it's just a matter of finding the heroes, or at least the non-villains, first.

For us, that meant setting up meetings with the principal and superintendent. After several long discussions, they both agreed to endorse the idea. They also helpfully informed us what the two hardest steps would be: getting the School Committee and the faculty to approve it.

The School Committee, a group of elected officials, was responsible for approving any major change or addition in the school. I already had plenty of experience with them through Project Sprout, much of it trying. But Project Sprout also gave me a leg up. I had once gone to the School Committee with a similar, if not quite as wacky, idea: that they should hand over a two-acre plot of land to a group of fifteen- and sixteen-year-olds, so that we could cultivate a garden and supply food to the cafeterias. But in the end, after a marathon meeting, and with a far-from-unanimous vote, they had approved Project Sprout on a trial basis.

Project Sprout was extremely successful. Three years after it was approved, the garden was twelve thousand square feet, with an additional acre of fruit production, a greenhouse, a farm stand, and a toolshed. Three days a week, Project Sprout food supplied the district's three cafeterias. Project Sprout had also become internationally recognized. This didn't mean the committee would definitely approve the Independent Project, but it did mean they might be more open to listening to crazy proposals from Mr. Huron and me.

It was the faculty, the superintendent and principal warned me, who would be most difficult to convince. This surprised me at first. The faculty had always been so supportive of the garden! But the idea of a student-run school sounded, from the get-go, like a threat to teachers. Were we saying teachers weren't needed? Were we trying to belittle their roles, or make them redundant? It's not surprising that this was their initial impression.

Second, people in any profession who have been doing something a certain way for a long time can be reluctant to change. Of course, not all teachers are wary of reform, but quite a few, understandably, are. This can make even the most minor changes to a school's curriculum almost impossible to enact. Mr. Huron, responsible for school scheduling, had for years been trying to convince the faculty to try out some different approaches to the school day—nothing particularly radical. He had suggested extending periods, or having a trial week at the start of the semester where students could preview classes. But his efforts were in vain. His proposals always became bogged down in bureaucracy, usually at the stage of the Curriculum Steering Committee—which didn't bode well for a change as big as the one we wanted to make.

The resistance Sam met with from teachers did not surprise me one bit. All my years of visiting classrooms, whether as a mom helping out with a holiday celebration, a researcher collecting data, or an adviser supporting teachers, have shown me the wide range of teachers working in high schools today. There are a few terrible ones—teachers who don't like teenagers, don't know much about their subject matter, are not smart, or have no idea how to help others learn. But terrible teachers are actually few and far between. I have also seen my share of really wonderful teachers—smart, knowledgeable, skilled professionals who love kids—teachers who bring the class alive, give feedback that changes a student's understanding, and give lively assignments that challenge kids of all abilities. However, the majority of teachers are like the rest of us—skilled in some ways, weak in others, teachers who want to do a good job. But most teachers, weak, strong, or in between, are deeply if unconsciously motivated to avoid stress, difficult challenges, and responsibilities that will make them feel bad about themselves.

Which is why, even in good schools with a good faculty, it is so very hard to get teachers to change. Whether it's a master teacher on top of his game or a struggling teacher who is barely controlling the classroom, the incentives and supports for making bold changes are low.

Faced with disappointing results (poor test scores, disinterested students, complaints from parents), teachers, and those who guide them, tend to push for small changes—use a textbook, don't use a textbook, give tests often, give them rarely, let students do homework in class, use class time for discussion only. Rarely do teachers consider the idea that the fundamental task of teaching should be reimagined. With a few striking exceptions, the basic model of what teachers should do, and what their relationship to students should be, has remained unchanged since the middle of the nineteenth century.

But there is another reason why so many on the curriculum committee seemed resistant to Sam's proposal. Years before, I knew a teacher at another school. We used to meet frequently, over coffee, to talk about how to improve his high school. This teacher was smart, well educated, and full of energy. He had a reputation as the dynamic, intense, excellent teacher, best suited to the most able kids. They read Plato and Thomas Friedman with him. They wrote essays answering tough questions. He demanded a lot of them and got a lot from them. If ever there was a teacher who seemed confident enough to consider new ideas, it was this guy. We had some terrific conversations, trading ideas about what kids should learn, good books they might read, what was wrong with the school administration, and so on. But when I began talking about all of the research showing that teenagers craved the chance to exert more control over their own academic lives, to make more of their own choices in what they studied and how they studied it, his long back stiffened, his head tilted back, and his deep voice got steely. He said, "I've been working with teenagers for fifteen years. I know them. I know what they want and need. I don't care what the research says. They can't make their own choices, and they aren't even happy when they do. They crave authority, and they need it."

At the time, of course, I had absolutely no inkling that Sam would someday be starting a student-run school. But what hit me like a cold blast of wind, sitting in that coffee shop, was the teacher's certainty that working with kids had taught him everything he needed to know about them. It seemed never to have occurred to him, a very smart and cultivated guy, that one's daily experiences often serve only to confirm one's preexisting ideas. Psychologists have shown time and again that people use daily encounters to confirm their biases rather than challenge them. Thus, for instance, if a teacher thinks kids are rarely motivated to learn on their own, they are likely to notice those moments when kids act bored, try to get away with little work, or resist difficult tasks. They are unlikely to notice the many signs that kids actually crave challenge and are eager to learn. To add to this dynamic, the teacher who assumes teenagers are not motivated to learn sets up situations that discourage intrinsic motivation (learning for its own sake), instead creating a class where the only possible motivation is extrinsic (a high grade, a free hall pass, a chocolate bar). Thus they form a classroom that, however subtly or invisibly, shapes young people to behave just as the teacher expects them to. Then they can turn to someone like me and say, "You see? These kids are only motivated by rewards." Or in the case of this particular teacher, "You see? They can't handle autonomy."

So I wasn't surprised by the varying types of resistance Sam met with. Teachers are not given much encouragement to try new things, to take risks, and to think about kids in new ways. In fact, events of the past fifteen years or so have pushed many of them into corners. Good teachers feel less and less freedom to do their thing. Weak teachers have felt scared and shamed. And in all the talk of education reform, the discussion has almost always centered on specific pedagogical techniques—almost never on the role teenagers could or should play in their own education.

When Sam proposed the Independent Project to the Curriculum Steering Committee, I thought back to that coffee shop exchange, seven years before. I couldn't change that smart teacher's ideas about adolescence. But maybe some adolescents could.

Most public schools have something similar to the Curriculum Steering Committee. In my school, it was made up of the principal and about ten teachers, and they had to approve any change to the curriculum *before* it went to the School Committee for final approval. Creating a new school within the school counted as a change to the curriculum, so the CSC would be my first port of call for approving the Independent Project.

Mr. Huron and I prepared for months, all the while checking in with the principal and superintendent to see where they thought we'd get hung up, so that we could be several steps ahead when it came to the first meeting. Lots of the details still weren't worked out in my own head. For example, the idea to regroup the traditional subjects didn't come to me until the August before the Independent Project started.

But I had worked out the basic tenets of the school and, with Mr. Huron's help, had started to figure out some of the logistics. Some of these logistics just came about practically. For example, how many students should the school have? In theory, the Independent Project could have three hundred kids (the whole high school had six hundred students) or two kids. I wanted to have a wide range of students, so that meant definitely more than two. And I figured the more kids, the more we would learn about whether the ideas worked. But I was also nervous. What if it was a disaster? It would really suck if it failed for a hundred kids. So the fewer students, the less guilt I would feel if it crashed and burned. I settled on ten.

Similarly, I thought the school could work for all students. But because freshmen and sophomores have more fixed requirements, and sophomores had to take statewide standardized content exams, I thought it would be a lot less messy if we limited the school to juniors and seniors. Plus, although *I* believed that high schoolers of any age were responsible enough to run their own school, in case I was wrong, it seemed less risky if we targeted older kids.

These are the kinds of things that started to fall into place as I began to build the school. They're different from the "design" stuff, because they're not part of a grand vision for the perfect school. I didn't think, "If I could design my dream school, it would be only for

seventeen- and eighteen-year-olds, not fifteen- and sixteen-year-olds."
It just made sense logistically.

So by the time I first presented to the CSC, I had a proposal with
the basic components worked out. The Independent Project would
be an alternative school within a school, run largely by students. To
start with, it would have around ten kids, although, hopefully, if it was
successful, it could grow. Legally, to be part of the public school, it
needed to track the regular school year and the regular school day. In
the afternoons, the students would focus on an Individual Endeavor,
and that would be the same all year, barring extreme circumstances.
In the mornings, we would do academics, focusing on the core disciplines: science, the humanities, math, and English.

In Massachusetts, you have to get a certain number of credits, some
of which have to be in particular fields, to graduate. You need four
English credits (so you have to take English every year), three math
credits, three science credits, two history credits, and so on. And you
need twenty-two credits overall, so you need to take a relatively full
load of classes every year.

This meant two things for my proposal. One, the students would
have to get a year's worth of credits for doing the Independent Project.
This was a given, because otherwise it wouldn't be part of the school.
If kids couldn't get credits for doing it, they couldn't do it (unless they
dropped out). Second, as far as I was concerned, students should get
a science, history, math, and English credit for doing the IP. This
seemed pretty obvious to me. The whole point of this was that it was
a replacement for regular school, in which kids would still learn the
traditional disciplines (albeit in a different manner). If it really was a
school within a school, then the work should merit the same credits.

So that was what I had going in. The bare bones of my vision. But
a real school—a brick-and-mortar, living, breathing school—is born
when a vision, or a dream, gets molded by reality. Thinking back on
the birth of the Independent Project, I often picture my vision for a
new school getting thrown down a chute filled with booby traps. The
thing that gets thrown in is untouched by the real world. But the chute

is filled with spinning blades, cookie-cutter molds, and chisels. These are the opinions of other people, rules, regulations, enemies, and logistics. As the vision passes down the chute, a corner gets chipped off here, a side caved in there. The bottom gets dented, the top blasted with spray paint. At some point, it gets forced through a cutout outline like a plastic extrusion, and some of it rebounds to its original contours but much of it is forever reshaped. And eventually it emerges at the other side of the chute, a new entity.

My vision was thrown into the chute during the first Curriculum Steering Committee meeting.

We met with the CSC three times in the spring of my junior year, with each meeting lasting about an hour, and each one separated by about two weeks from the one before it. In between the meetings I was supposed to address the concerns raised in the previous meeting and come back with an altered proposal. In some instances I did; in others I didn't.

In the very first meeting, a few things became abundantly clear very quickly. First, there were a few teachers who, almost without a doubt, were never going to approve a program like this. Yet there were also a few teachers who seemed, from the get-go, excited and ready to help make it happen. They had questions and concerns. But they thought that, in principle, it was a good idea. And they trusted Mr. Huron and me to execute it well. These were the teachers who became involved with the Independent Project later on.

The rest of the teachers—the majority of them—seemed on the fence. They were dubious but willing to listen and talk it out.

I said earlier that most teachers resist real change, and I offered some explanations for why. But as Sam has described, the teachers in his school responded to his proposal with a wide range of reactions. Quite a number shut him down right away. Not all of the naysayers were bad teachers. In fact, at least two of them were considered among the best teachers in the high school. They were knowledgeable and demanding and their students got high scores on AP tests. The school was proud of them, and the best students chose to take their courses. But they were rigid, tied to a way of doing things that worked for them and the comparatively small number of students who liked that approach—the AP students, for instance.

Others (just a couple, actually) embraced the idea with excitement, recognizing it as an invitation to do interesting work with students and happy to support something that fit with their hunch about what wasn't working. A select few of them were not one bit surprised that kids might have good ideas about their own education. This group included some of the most unusual and wonderful teachers in the school—among them two teachers who had the distinction of being equally terrific with the strongest students and those who were barely getting through high school. They were themselves very well educated, very confident of their own intellectual strengths, and, most of all, thought students had interesting things to say. These were teachers who not only loved students but also had a high regard for them.

But as Sam said, most of the teachers seemed alarmed and wary. Among this group were the teachers everyone has met. They were informed on their topics but only to a degree. They knew just a little more than the students, whether it was in English literature, geometry, or chemistry. Several of these teachers had a reputation for being jolly with kids, good at reining in the smart aleck, helping the newcomer find her way, and reaching out to the kid having trouble at home. Yet they faltered when a student didn't fit one of their categories (wiseass, shy kid, kid in trouble), and students who questioned their expertise made them uncomfortable. These were the same teachers who dreaded the involved parents as much as they disparaged the uninvolved ones. I have sat in many faculty lounges and heard the same conversation again and again. It goes something like this: "No wonder Joey struggles. I don't think his parents have looked at his homework once this year" (or "Alicia's mother is never home"; "Matt's family life is a mess"; "Irene's parents never say no to her"; and so on). They are discouraged by their students' fractured and inadequate parenting and feel sure it accounts for many problems that fall in their laps. They're not wrong.

Ironically, however, these teachers are even more undone by educated, vocal parents who assert their right to have a say in what goes on in schools. I know because I was one of those parents, and all the good breakfasts and sound sleep and field-trip chaperoning I provided my children with did nothing to offset the teachers' aggravation with my questions and concerns. One smart and talented English teacher told me that I had ruined her year because I asked her to explain to me the comments she had made on my son's papers—that I had undermined her self-confidence and that I should have kept quiet. When I told her my role was not to help her self-confidence but to help my son have a good education, she stopped speaking to me. These teachers seemed comfortable at school—they liked all the familiar routines. Which may explain why they were so uneasy at the thought of the Independent Project. What the teachers said, however, was simply that it all seemed too risky.

This part intrigued me. What exactly did they think might happen? I kept remembering a film that came out in 1968 called *Wild in the Streets*. In that film, hippies hell-bent on social revolution turned the political system (and the country) upside down. As a child, the sense that anarchy might be just around the corner, that crazy kids, high on LSD, might take over, was terrifying to me. As an adult, I kept thinking that some of the teachers in Sam's school reacted to his proposal as if it, too, would lead to *Wild in the Streets*, as if letting a small group of students do something different was dangerous, as if it might lead to all kinds of unimaginable badness. I kept wondering, as I sat on the sidelines listening to Sam's descriptions of those meetings, just what it was they thought might happen. Did they think the students would incite complete revolt among the other students? Did they think that the students in the Independent Project might suddenly unlearn all they knew and never again acquire an academic skill? Were they worried that the kids in the Independent Project might refuse to return to regular classes once the project had ended? And this led to the second mystery. It seemed, from what I heard, that they were particularly worried that kids would "lose ground" in key academic areas. That choosing and discussing books, or learning mathematics in a new way, would set them irrevocably off track. But if all their previous progress could be undone in a semester, what did that say about what they had learned before?

This concern, which is likely to face any group of kids who want to change their high school experience, is reasonable only on the surface. Naturally teachers want to make sure kids aren't painting themselves into a corner, digging themselves into a hole, or in other ways sabotaging their own educational progress. And yet, that worry is based on a faulty assumption—the assumption that the regular courses the students have been taking are working well. We have more than enough evidence showing that that is not the case.

Many students lose interest in learning while they are in high school. How do we know? Because too few students graduate and continue on to college. There is another even subtler way to measure the success of high school courses: the number of courses students want to take in college that are not simply utilitarian. Several recent reports show that students register for far more courses in economics and other job-oriented subjects than they do courses in literature, philosophy, physics, or mathematics. In other words, they don't develop a love of learning, or worse, they lose the love of learning they may have had as children. If conventional high school classes turn students off and push them away from more education, the courses are not working well. Second, as the US Department of Education, elite colleges, state universities, and community colleges have all seen, students are arriving at college without the academic know-how they need to even get by, much less do well. More and more colleges have to offer remedial courses, tutoring, and special workshops, and college professors have to take material out of the syllabus, assign less complex readings, and simplify the requirements, because students cannot keep up. One clear cause of this downward slide is that the courses currently taught in high school are not working all that well—which makes one wonder what it was those reluctant teachers on the Curriculum Steering Committee were so worried about giving up.

*   *   *

It became clear very quickly that the IP would never be approved for a whole year. It seemed like too much of a risk all at once. Why not try it for a month? Or a quarter? Why not make it an after-school program, so there's no risk at all! Either way, a year would never fly. I accepted that, partly because I didn't have a choice, but also because I had my own doubts and fears. How could I know if it would work?

However, I wouldn't make it a few weeks, or an after-school program. For this to work, it needed to be *real* school. If it was an after-school program, only the truly motivated kids would do it. That didn't interest me. And if it lasted only a few weeks, the students doing it would just use it as an opportunity to goof around. When I said this, a few teachers responded, "Aha! See! You admit they'll just goof around!" I had to explain that if you marginalized it, or made it too short, it would seem meaningless, like a vacation, and then most high schoolers (most anyone) would use it as an opportunity to do just that—take a vacation. But if you handed over their whole education to them and said, "Here, for the coming months, your education is in your hands," then it could become something more. So I agreed to make it a one-semester program.

Similarly, in the second meeting, the committee raised the question of credits. Some of the on-the-fence teachers said, "Well, why don't you have them do the IP for most of the day, but they can take regular English and math and meet their requirements." I wouldn't budge on this front. If the IP made up part of their day, but then they still had to do the "real" stuff, it would belittle the worth of the program. If they had homework for their other classes, they would end up doing that and not working on their Individual Endeavors. It would feel like their classes were real school, and the IP was free time. It would have to be the whole day, or it wouldn't be worth doing at all.

So, bit by bit, we worked through these logistics, and as we went through the process, some of the on-the-fence folks were gradually won over. I think this happened for two reasons. One, we made concessions (like making it only a semester) that took out some of the risk involved. And two, I think the more they heard Mr. Huron and me talk about it, the more an idea that had started out seeming radical and wild began to seem sensible and reasonable.

At some point in the second meeting, we came upon one of our biggest stumbling blocks, the matter of credits. Barring one or two teachers, no one thought we should get subject-specific credits for the Independent Project. This seemed really unfair to the students who would take part. "Yes, you can do the Independent Project, which is officially part of our school, but you'll have to double up on all your courses in the subsequent semester to make up for it."

I was able to win quite a few teachers over by explaining how we would approach academics. And for a while, I thought we might triumph. What I didn't foresee was the influence of the teachers' union. The union rep came down hard on this front: if we tried to award students subject-specific credits without having teachers teaching them those subjects, he would come down with the full force of the union. I didn't really know what that meant at the time, but afterward the principal explained that I should back off on that front. It was a battle not worth fighting.

So the students would get a semester's worth of credits. But they would be general credits, and they'd have to make up half an English credit and whatever other subjects they needed to graduate.

With that solved, we came into the final meeting. It was still about fifty-fifty at that point. There was really only one obstacle left to overcome. And that was to convince the CSC of the core tenet of the IP, the idea of its being student run. Of the three and half hours I spent with the CSC, two and half hours were spent trying to convince them that students wouldn't just use it as an excuse to mess around. Of course, I didn't have any proof. That's what the Independent Project was supposed to be. But I had to get it approved first!

While I was trying to make my case, one of the teachers in the "absolutely not" camp was getting more and more frustrated. He was actually visibly red in the face. Finally, he blurted out, "It's ridiculous to think that kids can be trusted to learn on their own!"

Interestingly, this teacher and I had always got along really well.

I loved his class, even though most people hated it, and I did really well in it. We didn't get along so well once I started the Independent Project.

Once I had convinced about half the teachers, or maybe a bit more, it was time to go to a vote. My final appeal was this: "If you think that our school works for everyone, if you think that everyone is benefiting from the way we do things now, and we're not failing anyone, then you shouldn't approve the Independent Project. Why fix something that ain't broke? But if you think we're coming up short, if you think we're letting a significant number of kids down, then why not give this a shot? I can't promise it will work, but I can promise if we try it, we'll be a little bit closer, one way or another, to doing the best for our students."

And it worked. I think the final vote was six to three, with some abstentions. The Independent Project was approved by the Curriculum Steering Committee to run as a pilot for one semester. After that, it would be reviewed and they would decide whether to make it a permanent school within the school.

We still had to go to the School Committee, but after facing the faculty, and with the CSC's, the principal's, and the superintendent's support, the School Committee was actually a lot less daunting. It took only two meetings to get its approval. And then my new school was officially a reality.

At seventeen, Sam was naïve. And he was brash. From the time he decided to do this, it never seemed to occur to him that he might not get past the first stage. I was forty-nine. I had failed many times and watched others, even those with wonderful ideas, never get past step one. But the great thing about seventeen-year-olds is that they're usually looking forward, sure that whatever they have imagined is just moments away from becoming a reality. It's one of the strongest features of adolescence, and one worth nurturing—that combination of certainty, urgency, and determination. Sam had it in spades. At their worst, teenagers push past people, talk too loudly, assume everyone thinks that they are as funny and fun as they feel. But the other side of this strangely exuberant egocentrism is that they can make things happen.

I was completely unsure, in those first few months, if Sam's proposal would make it past the committee meetings. I knew all the people, logistics, and institutional inertia that could stall it at any number of points. Sam, on the other hand, seemed blithely unaware that any problem could crop up that he couldn't overcome.

The process of the "dream school" passing through the chute can be really frustrating. So many things get changed, so many concessions made. But if you are able to keep the core tenets alive, in the long run, it's worth it. Because what comes out at the other end of the chute is a real school.

And now that *my* school was real, I needed to find its most important component: its students. This all started with wanting to make things better for my friends, who I felt were underserved by school. And my friends spanned the academic spectrum. That's one of the reasons I love public school. It's for everyone, regardless of background or ability. So I wanted my new school to be exactly the same. It should work for everyone, from students considering dropping out to students on their way to the Ivy League.

But we couldn't have more than ten kids. That was part of the deal. And we couldn't force kids to do it. So we had to have some kind of application process. We started by spreading information about the Independent Project. We distributed letters to all students describing the program and inviting them to apply. I talked it up among my friends and told them to spread the word. In his role as guidance counselor, Mr. Huron talked to the counselees he thought would benefit from the program, both students who were coasting by getting good grades without applying themselves and kids who were considering dropping out, for whom this might be a last hope. This was really useful, because it was how we hooked some of the students who later admitted to thinking the program sounded "stupid" when they first heard about it.

The truth is, we weren't really planning to reject anyone. We knew we would be lucky if ten kids applied. Students who were really worried about college would think it was too risky to try an experimental school in their junior or senior year. And lots of kids just wouldn't bother—they had accepted that high school was mostly boring and were biding their time until it finished.

So why have an application process at all? Three reasons. One, it would be a way to spread the word. Two, it would help legitimize the program, so that people wouldn't just absentmindedly sign up for it, treating it as a joke. And three, it would serve as a chance to give interested students an insight into what the program would be like. I knew that one of the challenges we would face would be helping students overcome all the bad habits and associations they had learned so far in school. So the earlier we started, the better.

In this way, the application was as much for incoming students as it was for us. I came up with three questions for students, and they could choose to answer them in writing or orally. The first question was: "If you could spend six months working on anything you wanted, what would it be?"

I knew that many of my friends had never even considered the idea of working on something for an extended period of time, or paused to think about what they would do if they *did* have free time. It's an alien concept, because it's never been an option.

During the CSC meetings, faculty members kept asking, "What about students who have no interests?" Well, I've yet to meet a high school student with *no* interests. Sometimes, they already have interests, but their interests don't fall into the relatively narrow arena of high school subjects. After all, most people don't spend their lives pursuing the subjects that are covered in high school. Perhaps even more commonly, they've never been given the opportunity to think about their interests, because they've spent so long being told what to learn.

This was the reason for our first question. To get prospective students to start thinking about what they might be interested in pursuing if they had a real opportunity to do so. Indeed, it *was* hard, at the start, for some students to think about what they would do, because no one had ever asked them. But every single student who has ever done the Independent Project ended up finding something to be passionate about.

The second question was actually a command: "List all of the uses for a stick." This was partly for fun. But it was also to get them to start thinking outside the box, to realize that the questions we would explore in the IP would be unlike anything they had done before. It's the kind of question that anyone, regardless of ability, can answer and push themselves with.

And finally, we asked them to consider a challenge they had faced in the past and explain how they overcame it. The purpose of this was partly to let them know that the Independent Project was going to be hard work. It's not easy to be responsible for your own education. But more important, it was to let them know that, in the IP, *they* would be responsible. No one else would swoop in to save them. They needed to be thinking about how they would overcome obstacles, not how someone else would do it for them.

By the time anyone is in their mid-twenties, a key part of life is figuring out when to work, when to relax, and how long it will take to complete certain tasks. Perhaps that's what teachers think they're teaching when they talk, which they do incessantly, about time management. In my experience this is completely off the mark. Kids who are very organized and goal oriented become so focused on managing their time that they give little thought to how they're actually *spending* their time. Which is why, when they get to a college like Williams, they schedule themselves up to the hilt, ticking off to-do lists and barely stopping to take in any of the experiences at their fingertips. Of course, there are many students who are not so put together and have no sense of how to apportion their time. They dawdle at dinner, watch too much TV, postpone their homework, and along the way forget essential assignments, materials, or even appointments. For those students, all the little tricks they are offered in the guise of "time management" hardly help. Telling kids how to manage their time for tasks they don't care about rarely works. Tell a young basketball player who falls asleep dreaming of the net how to warm up better before a game, and she'll remember that tip quickly and easily. But tell a kid who plays only because her parents make her, and she's unlikely to use the advice. In order for students to learn how to manage their time, they need to be working on things that matter to them.

By asking applicants, right away, to identify what they cared about, Sam was highlighting a key feature of the school—that students would need to manage their own time and they'd need to figure out what they actually wanted to spend their time doing. He couldn't have known this, but he was inviting them to begin the process researchers now consider essential for healthy development: acquiring a sense of purpose.

It's not unusual to ask students to submit applications in school. It's common for students to fill out forms or take tests in order to gain admission to AP courses or gifted-and-talented programs. In some cities students might need to apply in order to get into the "better" high schools. But in those situations, applications are used to sort out those who have potential from those who don't. Sam's application process was not selective in the usual sense. He wasn't interested in whether kids were smart enough, or even hardworking enough. He wanted them to take a first step in becoming more self-directed learners. To me, Sam's application process looked less like a barrier and more like an invitation—an invitation for teens to begin building their own paths, leading them from the world of childhood to the world of adulthood.

So that was it. The whole application. Mr. Huron suggested we get the parents involved early in the process. Anyone who wanted to apply had to get his or her parents' written permission. The thinking was that if it *was* a disaster, better that the parents were aware their kids were doing it and had given them permission to do it. Also, we figured, the more aware the parents were, the more support the students would get for it at home. We didn't want anyone's parent calling up furious that his or her child had no homework anymore.

We actually lost a few potential students early in the application process this way. It was common to hear, "I really want to do this, but my parents would never let me." This came both from students who wanted to go to Harvard and from students who were scraping by.

In the end, we were right to expect few applicants. Though dozens of students expressed interest, only eight students completed the application, including myself. And all eight of us were accepted.

We certainly did span the academic spectrum. We ranged from valedictorian to consistent Fs, and everything in between.

You would be hard-pressed to find a school in this country that didn't track students, one way or another. Separating students by ability and aspiration is so deeply woven into our educational system, it has become part of the fabric. Sit in on an AP class, almost anywhere in the United States, and you will find kids who stay quietly in their seats, keep their eyes on the teacher, write down their assignments, and raise their hands when a question is asked. Sit in on many CP (college prep, which is one euphemism for the less rigorous level) courses and you will see students talking when they are supposed to be listening, getting up to go before the teacher has given the assignment, and staring blankly when asked to contribute.

But the kids' classroom behavior is not the only thing that divides the academic tracks. Often the liveliest, most skilled, and best-educated teachers work in the AP classes, while the less adept or less educated teachers end up in the lower levels (as I mentioned earlier, this is not always the case). Finally, the work itself differs in almost every way. AP students are expected to do more, to read novels rather than excerpts, to write papers rather than fill in blanks, to solve mathematical problems rather than follow preset procedures.

Smart, academically able kids are often relieved to be in a class with others who want to work hard, who have good ideas, who read the book. And kids who struggle frequently prefer to be among others who struggle too, so they don't stand out when they fail the test. Yet ultimately, this system is bad for everyone. Research has shown that less able kids work and think at a higher level when they're around more able kids. The most able kids learn material more deeply when they have to explain it to others. Everyone benefits from figuring out how to work closely with people who are not like them. But mixing kids of different ambition and skill will not succeed if you keep everything else the same.

Right from the get-go, with its admissions procedures, the Independent Project focused on what all kids have in common and what all kids need: time to think about what they want to learn, an expectation that they could choose things that were challenging and interesting to them, and a demand that they take some responsibility for their own learning. Because the kids would choose their own questions and map out their own strategies for finding answers, they would, by design, be working on topics, tasks, and goals that fit their intellectual abilities. Because they worked together in a close-knit group (more close-knit than Sam might have expected, since in the end they had only eight kids that first year), their differences became a strength, not something to be avoided.

There isn't a kid around (at least within the typical population) who won't benefit from learning how to learn new things, form good questions, evaluate his or her own efforts, give help to others, take help from others, exchange views, and share knowledge. In this sense, the Independent Project represented the antithesis of tracking.

I made three assumptions when building my new school. The first assumption was that the school I wanted to build would be a reality. It was only later, when people asked me how I made the leap from thinking that high school should be different to actually starting a real school, that I realized it could have happened any other way. Designing a new school just for the sake of thinking about how to improve education didn't appeal to me. This was worth doing only if it was going to happen in the real world—if real, live students could experience a new kind of education.

My second assumption was that it was going to happen within the walls of my public high school. I've since talked to people who want to re-create the Independent Project, and they have asked me about starting charter schools or creating a homeschooling program, an after-school movement, or an online school. That never occurred to me. I wanted things to be better for my friends and classmates. So, in my mind, it was always going to be part of my public school, and it was going to be available to everyone.

And finally, though I knew my school's curriculum would look unlike anything in traditional school, I assumed that, physically, my school would look like any other. When I daydreamed about my senior year, I pictured a classroom with a chalkboard and a whiteboard and desks and posters on the walls.

By the end of my junior year, we had the school district's approval and we had our students. All that was left was finding a space for the school, which, I figured, would be easy. There were eight of us, so we needed only one classroom. I'd just pick the nicest one with the most sunlight!

Of course, it wasn't so simple. The school wouldn't give us a classroom. They needed to use all the rooms for regular classes. They offered to find an empty room for each of the eight periods of the day; we could just move every time the bell rang. No way. The students couldn't feel like an add-on whose needs were secondary to the rest of the school, shoved around at the whim of the other classes. Also, we were trying to abolish arbitrary periods and divisions, to have our schedule be fluid and natural. If we had to get up and move every time the bell rang that feeling would be ruined.

So they offered us the band equipment room. As long as we didn't mind hearing the music lessons all day and having students come in each period to get their instruments, it would be perfect!

No, thanks. Mr. Huron and I found an abandoned farm stand across the street that was on school property. We had built things together for Project Sprout. We could spend the summer fixing it up and insulating it!

It didn't meet health and safety requirements. There was a separate building by the tennis courts that had been used by a special education group but was now out of commission. Could we use that? It would be perfect! Like a little schoolhouse!

The school didn't want us that far away.

I understood why Mr. Huron and Sam were so intent upon finding just the right space. They wanted a room of their own. They knew that the Independent Project had to be more than a few special classes, or a replacement for afternoon electives, in order to have the transformative impact they were seeking. Even the most well-meaning and supportive members of the school—the principal, the superintendent, and some of the more enthusiastic teachers—didn't really get it. They assumed that as long as Sam and Mr. Huron had use of some classrooms some of the time, they should be able to do what they had envisioned. That was based, at best, on a misunderstanding of the scope Sam had in mind. I knew this right from the beginning, because when I ran into various staff members from the school, they'd say something nice, like, "It's so great that Sam wants to do this awesome independent study," or "We heard Sam is beginning an independent project—that's great." It's amazing how important an article such as "an" or "the" can be. I knew from that seemingly meaningless slip that they didn't get it. They thought that he was adding one more interesting option to the range of courses, independent projects, and activities they already offered, another item on an à la carte menu. They didn't fully see that this was actually a prix fixe meant to replace their old menu.

A group of kids who want to start their own school can do it in any number of settings, but they do need a space of their own. The space doesn't determine what happens in it (that is up to the students and the people who support their efforts). But having a distinct place dedicated to the new school embodies one of the central ideas we are talking about: that kids have ownership over their own educational experience. Whether a classroom, an unused counselor's office, a screened-off section of the library, a little-used woodworking room, or a small building somewhere on school grounds, four walls and a door are essential. They announce to everyone—the faculty, the administration, the parents, and the other students—that the student-run school has substance, in every sense of the word. The school must take shape. But *what* shape it takes will depend on the kids who start it, the existing school, and the community, as well as the locale itself (city, rural, suburban, crowded, sparse, etc.). Some schools have space to spare, and others do not. All students will benefit, as Sam did, from having to figure this part out. The search to find a place, and the students' right to stake out their ground, is a vital part of the process.

Some students will start a school for five kids, and others may start one for fifty. Some kids will start with a full year's program; others will make it the fall term only. The details are important, but that doesn't mean they have to be the same in each setting, for each group of students. One of the things that makes a student-run school so compelling is that each group of students must figure out what they need to create a program that works for them and for the larger community. We know now that children do best when their families have homes. It's the same with a school, no less so for one run by students. They, too, need a home of their own.

I could see Sam pushing back against the subtle efforts to contain him or rein in his ambitions for the project. Each time the administration tried, in one way or another, to shrink what he had in mind, or keep his plans from breaking too far away from the regular structure, I held my breath a little, wondering who would win this silent battle of wills.

Mr. Huron and I spent the whole summer looking for a location for our school. Long after we had accepted our students, sent home letters, held an informational Q and A for parents, and gathered the group to make pizza and start to get to know one another, we still didn't have a physical school. It's funny, really, if you think about it. We went through all this bureaucracy to get the school approved, they finally said yes, and then they had nowhere to put us. Throughout that summer, Mr. Huron and I would call each other with ideas. "I've got it!" I'd say. "The auditorium!" "Already asked," Mr. H would say. "Spring musical gets priority." It became a joke between us. We'll go to school in the garden! And build fires in the winter! We'll construct a tepee in the hallway!

I thought Mr. Huron was making another joke when he finally told me where we could put the school. He called one day in August. "Well, I've got good news and bad news," he said. "The good news is that the school has offered us a space for the school that can be our own, and we can use it all day long without interruption." "Awesome!" I said. What could the bad news be? "Well," he said. "You're not gonna like where it is."

It was the coach's office in the girls' locker room.

We have good news and bad news too. The beauty of the kinds of changes we're talking about is that they can take almost any form, anywhere in the world. Your new school could have a thousand students or five students. You could construct a beautiful building with great facilities or plop the students in a locker room. These changes, unlike many popular educational reform proposals, don't require elaborate equipment, expensive new technology, complex schedules, or even abundant resources. They just need one really powerful, invaluable, irreplaceable resource. Kids.

That's the good news. Though Sam was shocked to find out they'd be in the girls' locker room, it was actually one of the wonderful things about the program. It didn't matter where they were—they didn't need computers, a library, a SMART Board, or even a chalkboard! They needed one another, and their own space to think and work and learn. Likewise, if you're starting your own school, based on some of the same principles we've discussed, you can do it anywhere, in any form.

The bad news is that you will, almost without fail, face many of the same difficulties as Sam. People are reluctant to allow change. Committees and school boards will balk; teachers will fight you; you will make enemies and maybe even lose friends. That is part of the process of building. Don't be deterred. Be flexible and reasonable. The goal is to make this work. But the key is knowing the difference between the elements that are immutable because they embody your educational ideas, and those that can be adjusted.

There are great classrooms and schools all over the world that function in the most unlikely settings and do things in an unexpected way. There is no really strong reason why a school committee should refuse a well-thought-through school that better serves the needs of its students and takes nothing away from the existing system.

And the trial of building your school will be worth it. If you've followed these steps, you're now standing in the coach's office of the girls' locker room. Or you've cut the ribbon on your new building. Or you've cleared out space in your attic. There are five of you, or fifty. You meet in the fall term, the spring term, or all year long. There isn't only one right kind of space or a crucial number of students. It's essential only that you have an educational idea and a plan for how to put that idea into action, and that you've worked out the basic logistics, so that you can coexist with others in your community. Now comes the fun part.

Your first day of school.

4

YOUR FIRST DAY

*Most of us have had some variation of the naked-on-the-first-day-of-school
dream. That's probably because, for most of us, the first day of school is a little
exciting and a little scary. Will we make friends? Will we like our teachers?
Will we embarrass ourselves or stand out in our first lessons? Will it be too
hard? Boring? Who will we sit next to on the bus? For us, at least, this mixture of excitement and fear never went away completely, though with each
passing year of school, from kindergarten up to senior year, it abated a little.*

*For Sam, however, that changed in his senior year of high school. Because
that first day was not just his first day of a new school year, but the first day
of a new school. The Independent Project. And so, for you too, there will likely
be a mixture of emotions on your first day. The most prominent one will be
anxiety.*

*You've done all this work, first deciding to start a new school, then designing
it, and finally building it, and today it actually begins. What if it's a disaster?
What if you let down your students? What if you were wrong about changing
the way school is run, and your experiment crashes and burns?*

*In this chapter we talk about the first day of the Independent Project, and
the week of orientation, or de-orientation, that followed, and why what happens in those early days is so important.*

I remember walking through the maroon doors of my public high
school the first day of the Independent Project, scared shitless. It had
finally dawned on me just how stupid I had been. I had spent my junior
year convincing the faculty and School Committee to allow me to run

an alternative school within a school, when I had absolutely no idea whether it would work at all. For all I knew, it could be a total disaster. In fact, I thought in my increasingly anxious mind-set, it probably *would* be a total disaster! I should have just left things as they were. I should have spent my senior year cutting class after lunch to go get ice cream and steal lawn ornaments with my friends. Instead, the fate of eight students' high school education was now at stake.

I had arrived an hour before school started, because Mr. Huron and I had a job to do. We had decided it wouldn't be fitting to start our new school by telling the students where to be. How could we start something radical on conventional footing? If the students arrived and we told them to go to their room and began taking attendance, it would send the wrong message. I wanted, from the moment they walked through the school doors, to be sending the message that everything would be new and different.

So instead of leading them to the girls' locker room, we let them find it. We created a scavenger hunt that took them all around the school, with clues taped on the stage, under a lunch table, on the door to the principal's office. While everyone else was bustling around, noses in their schedules, reading off room numbers and times (8:49, Chemistry, Room B52), our students were wandering around, working together to solve a scavenger hunt. They would arrive not at some arbitrary time (first period, 8:07) but whenever they had managed, as a team, to solve the clues. And the final clue, of course, would lead them to the girls' locker room.

Meanwhile, Mr. Huron and I waited in a small, ten-foot-by-ten-foot room that smelled, well, like a locker room. All it contained was a table, nine chairs (which Mr. Huron and I had lugged in earlier in the summer), and a rack of basketballs. The only windows led into the girls' locker room, and they had, of course, been blacked out. Sitting in the drab, beige-colored room with its fluorescent lighting, my hopes weren't very high.

"Relax," Mr. Huron said, and I tried.

Eventually, the students arrived, each of them with their mouths slightly agape. "Is this really where we're going to school this year?" said Tim, looking around. He was tall and lanky, with dark curly hair and a round face. His mother was Korean and his father American, and his skin was a very light tan. He had moved to our school two years earlier, and he had become part of my friend circle. He was funny, bright, and very talented. The short music videos and skateboarding films he put on YouTube were watched by almost everyone in school, and it was not uncommon to hear his beats coming out of someone's headphones. But despite his quick wit and abundant talent, he had struggled to excel in school. I would learn, in the coming months, that this was largely because, though he did well *in* class, outside of school he would always focus on music and film production over homework.

"Welcome to your new home," said Mr. Huron.

There was a pause, during which I worried that they would just turn and walk out, straight back into traditional classes. Luckily, Dakota spoke up. Dakota, whom I knew from her work on Project Sprout, was a small, short-haired girl, boyish but attractive. Her mind was like a razor, and she had coasted through school with relatively good grades without ever applying herself. She had a dry sense of humor that was unusual in high school and made her stand out. She could have been a good-looking member of the Addams Family. In her usual monotone voice, not really looking at anyone as she spoke, she said, "Excellent." Everyone laughed. And I began to relax.

A lot happened that first day. We started with an activity that eventually became part of our daily routine. We called it check-in. Everyone would take turns saying how they were doing, what was going on in their lives, what was new, and, in the beginning, what had happened over the summer. That first day, Mirabelle pointed out that "check-in" used to be a regular part of the day in elementary school, but disappeared from the schedule at some point during middle school. Why? Our lives outside of school have a huge impact on our lives inside of school. If your dog died yesterday, you're never going to be as productive today as you will be, hopefully, tomorrow. Having your peers and colleagues aware of your home life can only help. It also allowed us to start to get to know one another, and as the Independent Project progressed, it became a time to talk about our work and our passions. Being connected to and involved with one another's work and interests made us more effective at collaborating and pushing one another.

Sam met one of his best friends when he was two, in the day care program they both attended. In fact, his friend told me not long ago that he can still remember when it was diaper-changing time, and the two of them would be hoisted up on the table to get "powdered up." By the time they were thirteen they had befriended another boy who joined their school in seventh grade. In high school the three of them were inseparable. They went through everything together: missing the cut on teams, winning championships, meeting girls, breaking up, smoking pot, sledding, writing good papers, writing bad papers, getting into a brawl in town, applying to college, going to prom. There wasn't one important step in adolescence that they didn't take together, in one way or another. Yet they weren't alike: they didn't fall for the same girls, they weren't good at the same sports, they took different classes in school, and they had very different aspirations. Their bond with one another didn't simply transcend those differences—it fed on them. They each seemed to have more options, more dimensions, a fuller life, because of one another.

If you think about your own teenage years (whether they are happening now or happened thirty years ago), what comes to mind most vividly? Chances are, the best moments—those when you felt most alive, vigorous, joyous, and strong—involved friends. We now know that social connections are essential to well-being. When you feel closely connected to others, you can face almost anything. When you feel isolated from others, it's hard to thrive. But this is never more true than during the teen years. If you think about it for a minute, it makes complete sense. Though friendships matter in childhood, the central bond is still with one's parents and other family members. In adulthood, one's closest bonds tend to be with a romantic partner and one's children. In adolescence, when teens have left the circle of childhood and are not yet in the circle of adulthood, Lewin's "marginal men" turn to the other marginal men and women—their peers.

Earlier I described the beeper study by Csikszentmihalyi and Larson and talked about how disengaged and listless the kids felt during much of their everyday routines. But they weren't always bored. The diaries the teens kept made it as clear as daylight that they felt best when they were doing things with their friends. A recent wave of research on social media and their impact on the inner lives of teens provides an intriguing clue about this. It appears that though Facebook often gives teenagers a momentary feeling of sociability and connectedness, when they go offline they feel even more lonely than they did before. In other words, even now, in the age of the Internet, nothing replaces being with flesh-and-blood friends, in real time and space, doing real things together.

We all know the downside of adolescent friendships: teens egg one another on to take stupid risks, to try drugs, drink, have sex, drive fast, and skip class. And those worries aren't crazy. In one experiment, teenagers were asked to play a computer game that allowed for a variety of moves ranging in their level of riskiness. When teenagers were alone in the laboratory, they played it safe, choosing the low-risk moves. However, when there were other teens in the room, the subjects began veering toward the riskier options. They did this even though the other teens were quiet and did not play the game themselves. It seems that just the presence of peers has a powerful impact on teenagers, and it's not always a good impact (for instance, when a teen drives faster than she should because her friends are in the car with her). But there's another way to look at those data. The experiment shows that teenagers spur one another to action, which can be a good thing just as easily as it can be bad. What if being with pals incites a student to try a kind of fiction writing he's never tried before, or to come up with new interpretation of a historical event?

Harry Stack Sullivan, a prominent psychologist in the middle part of the twentieth century, argued that preteens use friendship to get relationship practice (how to confide in one another, give feedback, or respond to the emotional needs of someone else). More recently, researchers have shown that friendships and romantic relationships in adolescence provide further rehearsal for adulthood, giving teenagers essential practice for becoming spouses and parents.

Taken together, the studies make one thing very clear: happiness during the teenage years rises and falls with the success of one's social bonds. And it's not only that teens are happier when they can spend a lot of their time with friends. Time spent with friends is often time well spent, because it gives teens a chance to develop skills that are key to a happy adult life.

Why wouldn't educators want to build on the emotional and intellectual energy kids at this age provide for one another? Instead of relegating social interactions to the edges of the educational process, why not bring them to the center? If students could talk to one another in class, and if they were encouraged to share personal experiences as a prelude to sharing ideas and knowledge, as they did during Sam's check-in, maybe their intellectual experiences would seem more vibrant to them, and maybe they'd be less itchy to end class and get back to the hallways, cafeterias, and bathrooms.

Sam may have stumbled onto the check-in as a way of getting his group started, but he stumbled onto something worth keeping. That first check-in introduced the group to a concept that lay at the core of the IP: in this new model, friendship would become an ally rather than an impediment to learning.

That first check-in was longer than later ones, and because of the scavenger hunt, the rest of the school's first period ended while Mirabelle was telling us about her summer. Mirabelle was a lively and energetic student, with lustrous brown hair and blue-gray eyes. She was passionate about various things outside of school (including Project Sprout, which she had worked on since she was a freshman) but not very interested in academics. She had trouble focusing and sticking with things, and though her grades were fine, she often struggled, particularly in math and sciences. She had a self-diagnosed math phobia.

She was telling us about her trip to Africa when the first-period bell rang. She stopped midsentence, and everyone began to push their chairs back and get up. Tim may even have made it to the door. Then there was a pause. Everyone froze, a little awkwardly, not knowing what to do.

"No periods here, guys," I said.

"Jesus," said Dominic, in his high-pitched voice. Dominic had long, wavy blond hair and very light blue eyes, and often looked like he was in a daze. His voice was strikingly high and commanded attention in an unusual way, and his adventurousness and fun sense of humor meant he had lot of friends at school. Unfortunately, he was severely dyslexic, and he failed many of his classes. On top of his learning difficulties, he bucked at any sign of authority and was disgusted by arbitrary rules. Until he signed up for the Independent Project, dropping out had been a serious possibility (with his friends and his place on the soccer team being the main things that had kept him in school so far). "We're like sheep," said Dominic, and everyone laughed.

For the rest of the day, when a bell rang, people would cut off in the middle of a sentence or start to put things away and shuffle outside, before realizing there was nowhere else to go. It took us a long time to outgrow the long-ingrained habit of dropping everything at the sound of a chime.

But that's exactly why we had a week of de-orientation: so that we could undo some of the bad that had been done, and open up to some new ways of working, thinking, and learning. I believed that all kids could work hard, be curious, be passionate about learning, focus on their interests, collaborate, push one another, teach one another, and be responsible for their education. But I created the de-orientation week because I also knew that they had spent a dozen or more years being told what to learn and how to learn it; being encouraged to work in isolation, to not ask questions out of turn, to not critique peers, to learn but not teach, and being told that being interested in what they were learning was not particularly important. And I figured those twelve years could not be undone in a heartbeat.

The very first step in de-orientating was to read a children's story. Mostly I wanted us to do things together, and so for the rest of the week we'd be doing games and exercises. I wasn't the teacher, I wasn't in charge, and I didn't want to lead the whole time. But I knew the transition would have to be gradual. So I thought it was okay to start with me reading a story.

The book was *Many Moons*, by James Thurber. It's about a little princess who becomes ill, and a desperate king who will do anything to make her better. The princess says that the only thing that will make her well again is having the moon. The king seeks the help of all his most intelligent and powerful men—the mathematician, the magician, and the wise man—and yet none of them can come up with a solution. The king is entirely bereft, until the court jester comes along and suggests the king ask the little princess how to get the moon. The little princess provides an ingenious solution; she says that the moon is made of gold and is the size of a thumbnail, and so the king has the moon made for her. But then the king realizes that she will see the real moon in the sky that night, and again he asks all his wisest men what to do. None of them has a solution, and again the king is completely beside himself, until, once again, the court jester suggests the king ask the princess. The princess deftly explains that, just like when you cut a fingernail and a new one grows back, the same is true of the moon, and everyone is happy.

I read them that story for a few reasons. First, because sometimes the people who are supposed to have all the answers, like teachers or the wise men, don't. And sometimes the established methods for gaining those answers (the king asking the wise men, traditional schooling) are misguided. And sometimes, the someone who has the right methods (the court jester) or the right answer (the little princess) surprises us. Most important, it is only through the interplay of those two elements—the clever method from the court jester and the clever answer from the princess—that we can move forward. In the Independent Project, we had to be both the court jester and the little princess.

We also read the story because I loved the idea of starting this new school on a note of fiction. One of the things we were going to try to achieve in the coming semester was to get all of us, if we hadn't already, to fall in love with reading. Although I worried that starting with a children's story would make it seem like I was dumbing things down, or that we wouldn't be pushing ourselves, my concern turned out to be misguided. Though we read many more books, some of them by Faulkner, Wilde, and Vonnegut, the moon remained, always, our unofficial logo.

In his classic novel *Fahrenheit 451*, Ray Bradbury tells a cautionary tale about the threat of censorship. I have always loved the story, but oddly, whenever I think of it, what comes to mind is not from the book itself, but from Truffaut's film version. The movie ends with an indelible scene in which all the characters are wandering around together, quietly reciting to themselves the book they've each chosen to memorize. They are doing this as an act of defiance—even if the pages are incinerated, what is on those pages cannot be stolen from them. But the political message of the book was never that vivid to me. Instead, even as a child, I had a very personal interpretation. For me, the scene captured the allure of becoming one with a book. I always imagined each of those characters finding such solace or pleasure in a book that they would literally make it part of themselves. I assumed that those characters felt the way I did: reading was not just a means to knowledge, but a delicious end in itself. I was a college student before I realized that all the other kids did not feel that way.

And for the last thirty-five years, ever since I graduated from college myself, I've been trying to figure out why schools have such an amazing knack for ruining the one activity that is probably most important to the educated mind: reading. I've come to realize the main reason is that teachers simply don't give students enough stories to read. Far too much time is spent on turgid, badly written textbook passages, and not nearly enough time is given over to reading good fiction. It is true that some highly educated people prefer nonfiction, and it is true that by adulthood it is important to read newspapers, history, instructions, essays, and policy statements. But the roots of literacy lie in narrative. Children tell and listen to stories long before they have any sense of the written word. And the way into literacy is through stories—the stories parents tell their children about the past, and the stories children tell one another (some true to life, some completely made up). Research from psychology and anthropology is quite clear on this—everyone everywhere in the world tells stories, and virtually all children like stories. We know, too, that stories are not only powerful and useful for the very young. Narrative continues, even in adulthood, to be the primary way that people make sense of the world and themselves, impart information to one another, and build up a shared culture.

Eavesdropping on Sam as he planned that first day was a vicarious thrill for me. Long before, in the years when I taught elementary school, one of my favorite parts of teaching was to come up with fresh and intriguing ways to introduce a new learning activity. I wanted to surprise my students into thinking in a new way. I've never liked preset curricula, always drawn to the fun of coming up with something new. My ideas for teaching often came to me in the car, at breakfast, or as I walked down to get the mail. They were never very deliberate or studied.

I am pretty sure that like my younger self, Sam was going partly on instinct. His hunch was that if he read something delightful to the other students, something he loved, he would begin the process of luring them into a new affinity for fiction. He chose *Many Moons*, I think, because it was whimsical yet profound. I have no idea if it mattered to him that the author, James Thurber, was one of the twentieth century's masters of prose. But to me, this deceptively simple activity, reading something he loved to his friends, offered a whole new possibility for high school curricula—he was making books the spine of the educational experience.

It has never made any sense at all to me that although reading is the most important intellectual habit you can acquire in school, students typically encounter only a handful of captivating short stories and novels during their whole four years in high school. Some have argued that as long as kids become real readers, everything else will fall into place.

Sam added a twist to that idea, making reading a deeply social part of the day right from the start.

One day during de-orientation everyone had to teach the group something. Mirabelle taught us how to make sandwiches, Tim taught us how to give a good massage, Sarah taught us how Pixar animates its films, and Dominic taught us how to whittle a spoon. Many of them had never really taught anything to other students. They had all given presentations before, but that's very different from real teaching. Usually, when you give a presentation in class, the purpose is to test how well *you* know the material. But in our case, we had to make sure that, by the end of the lesson, each of the other seven students could actually do the thing that we were teaching. The real test here was how well the group learned.

Teaching was something we were going to be doing a lot of in the coming semester, so I figured it would be good to start with simple skills like making a paper airplane. Better to start by teaching something simple very well than teaching something complex poorly.

Then, after each person taught the group, everyone else had to go around and make one truly negative statement about that person's teaching.

"Tim, you did a lot of demonstrating, but you didn't let us practice it enough—it's difficult to learn just from watching."

"Sarah, you used a lot of jargon that maybe you know well but we don't, so it was tricky to follow at times."

Giving a peer harsh criticism is really hard, especially within a group you don't know very well. But if we were going to push each other and hold each other up to high standards in the coming semester, we needed to start practicing giving and receiving tough feedback.

Over the last ten years or so, whenever I visit a school, I've noticed that on some wall the administration has put up a mission statement, a list of goals, or a motto identifying key values. Some say "Try your best" or "Aim high"; some say "A love of learning" or "Mutual respect"; and some include a focus on citizenship. Though the proclamations vary somewhat, there is one thing they all include in one version or another. Every single school espouses the idea that they are a "community of learners." Though I see that written everywhere, here is what I see when I actually visit classrooms: a roomful of young people watching a teacher, a whiteboard, or a computer screen. However, a group of individuals all learning at the same time from the same source does not constitute a community.

I have seen many classrooms where students are invited or commanded to work together—sometimes pairs are poring over a math sheet; sometimes teams are building models of molecules or planning a presentation on a period of history. They are working together, helping one another complete a project. Here is what I virtually never see: students actually learning *from* one another. So it's not totally clear to me what makes those classrooms of people communities of learners, rather than just groups of students.

Becoming a community of learners takes deliberate work, effort, and practice. As every teacher knows, it's challenging to teach someone else something. Sometimes you know the material so well you find it hard to make it easy for a novice. Sometimes you don't know it well enough to explain it (or show it) to another. Knowing what to say to help another person improve her work is tricky. Trickiest of all is learning how to get real help from others. When teachers give criticism about a paper, test, or presentation, students can either tune out (as many do) or listen. When they listen, it's usually for one of three reasons: they feel they have to, they want a good grade, or they genuinely want to improve and trust the teacher to help them do so. Either way, most students assume that they must accept feedback from the teacher.

Here's what they don't learn from such interactions: how to be part of a group of people who learn together. I have noticed in my classes at Williams that it makes students very uncomfortable to challenge one another in a serious way. They think it's rude, or that it will in some way interfere with their friendships outside of class. And yet, by the time they graduate, if they don't know how to actually be part of a community of learners, they will stagnate.

It seems to me we give children far too much practice taking feedback from authority figures and not nearly enough practice giving and getting feedback from their equals. But I'll be honest. When Sam told me he was going to insist, that first day, that everyone say something negative about the other students' teaching, I was thinking, "Oh, Sammo. That's not gonna happen." He was so idealistic. He didn't know how intellectually reluctant most kids are. They'd rather be quiet than go out on a limb. Students wouldn't want to seem "mean." The kids from AP classes, I was sure, wouldn't want to make the vocational students feel bad. The kids with bad grades wouldn't want to sound pushy telling a smart kid what she did wrong. They were probably all so sick of criticism, the last thing they'd want was to create any themselves. I thought, "You're gonna hit a wall with this one, buddy."

On the other hand, I agreed with him that for the school to have any lasting impact, students would have to learn how to learn from one another. And when he described the particular students in the group to me, I suddenly realized something else. By giving one another feedback about their teaching, they would all step onto common ground. Whoever was doing the teaching (smart kid, struggling kid, A student, near dropout) knew more than the others about his or her topic. And none of them had ever been teachers before. Here was something they couldn't do without one another, and which none of them were particularly good at to begin with.

Since we were going to spend the first part of the semester working in the sciences, I designed a game related to asking questions. For most of us, for most of our education, questions had been discouraged. They were often disruptions, especially when a teacher felt pressured to cram through a lot of material in a short period. Answers reigned supreme, and if you could get the answers without asking questions, then you were really ace. Further, to the degree that questions had ever been encouraged (perhaps more often when we were younger), they were treated as peripheral, a necessary shortcut to an answer—"Feel free to interrupt with questions." "There's no such thing as a bad question."

In the Independent Project, questions were going to be more important than answers. In fact, rather than peripheral, questions would be central. Because knowing how to ask good questions and how to use them to guide your search for answers was much more important than knowing a bunch of answers. And that empty saying about there being no bad questions was just wrong, another way to trivialize the importance of questions. (Imagine how a hardworking author would feel if you said there's no such thing as a bad book.) Questions do differ in their quality, and learning how to construct a good one is essential to becoming a better learner.

The game I designed was simple. One person leaves the room. The rest of the group agrees on something about that person (say, the name of his dog) that no one in the group knows. When the person comes back in the room, everyone else is trying to find out that fact about the person, but they can't ask the question directly. The person is trying to find out what the others are trying to find out. If the group gets the answer (Rover) to their question first, they win. If the person figures out their question ("You're trying to find out my dog's name") before they learn the answer, he wins.

It's a simple, fun game, but it served several purposes. One, questions were going to be important in the IP, more important than answers. In the game, the dog's name doesn't really matter; what matters is coming up with questions that are cleverly constructed to find the answer without revealing intent. The person who left the room is trying to sift through the questions being asked to find out the real question that they are circling. The more you play the game, the more you learn about questions.

And that was the second purpose. Before then, we had rarely been asked to think about the construction of questions. But as we played, we were forced to think about the differences between what and how questions, about the value of broad versus specific questions, about how different questions lead to different answers. And finally, the game got us to start *practicing* the art of asking questions.

When I tell people I study curiosity in childhood, I virtually always get the same response: "Oh, how fascinating. It's so important. It's the key to learning." I've yet to run into an educator who says, "Curiosity is dangerous. It should be suppressed." And yet, a close look inside most classrooms will show that curiosity is rarely encouraged. Often it isn't even tolerated ("I'll answer that later"; "This is not a good time to raise your hand"; "That's not the topic we are discussing today"; "We don't have time for questions"). As Sam said, even when teachers welcome a question, they see it as a door to an answer, or a nice reminder that some of the students are actually interested in the topic. Rare is the classroom where teachers treat questions as the topic, helping students learn the difference between the strong and weak form of a question, or between questions that can be answered with data and those that cannot (the difference between "Which political party is better?" and "Which political party has reduced the crime rate?").

Research shows that by the time children are preschoolers they are determined investigators—they use questions to get answers they desperately want about the natural and social world. But when they get to school they ask far fewer questions and receive far fewer answers to the questions they most care about. It's safe to say that whatever they learned when they were three about how to ask a good question is the last time they get some guidance about how to inquire. Students who go on in academia must pick up where every three-year-old left off, figuring out the best way to frame a question and how to go about answering it. Why wouldn't this be something we'd teach in high school?

The Independent Project room looked like a photograph that had been desaturated, sapped of all its color. The room's walls were drab beige. There was a drab beige table, with hard plastic chairs around it. There was a drab beige locker-room-tile floor. The lights were fluorescent and horrible. It was just really, really ugly.

This drove Mirabelle crazy. She couldn't imagine spending a semester holed up in this shithole. So she ordered all of us to bring in
whatever decorations we could get our hands on at home. Dominic
brought an old lamp; I brought a rug I found in my garage. Everyone
brought in books from home so that we could establish our own library. Slowly the room started to fill with appealing, cozy objects and
artifacts. Still, the decorations didn't solve the problem of the world's
dullest walls. So Mirabelle decided we would paint a mural. Though
many of us (the worst culprit being me) were terrible artists, Mirabelle, Sarah, and Tim were gifted enough and, regardless of mural
quality, painting it was loads of fun.

But it was more than just fun. None of us had ever had the chance
to have a say over how our school looked. Maybe in elementary school
we had been tasked with cutting out turkeys at Thanksgiving, which
were then hung around the classroom. Or, in one or two truly excep-
tional high school classes, we were allowed to decide how the desks
were arranged. But let's be honest: that's pretty minor. In fact, looking back, it's funny to think that choosing our desk layout was ever a
big deal to us.

Now, in the Independent Project, we were being allowed to literally paint the walls how we wished. A small thing, perhaps, in and of
itself, but part of something bigger, and something essential, which
would only grow as time went on. For the first time in our lives, we
had control over meaningful aspects of our education. And though
it was taking a little while to get comfortable with, we were already
starting to love it.

Perhaps our best addition to the room was turning one of the walls
into an object-based group journal. It was already decided, as part of
our assessment, that everyone had to keep two journals for the en-
tirety of the Independent Project: one for academics and one for Individual Endeavors. But someone during that first week suggested we
should also have a collective journal. So we divided one of the walls
into sections, one for each week of the semester. At the end of each
week, everyone had to attach something to the wall that captured that

week for him or her. I think it was Tim who coined the name: the Encoded Story Wall of Time.

When I heard about Tim's "Encoded Story Wall of Time," a crazy re-
frain kept going through my head, "Hmm, which do I choose? Encoded
Story Wall of Time or SWiBAT Wall of Time? Or SWiBAT?" And each
time I thought of it I wanted to laugh out loud at the absurdity of the
contrast. For those who are not familiar with some of the newer techniques in schools across the country, SWiBAT is a common acronym,
used to make sure that teachers and children stay on task, and that students understand what they are supposed to be learning. The acronym
stands for "students will be able to." The idea behind it is reasonable
enough. One way to make sure teachers make good use of the time
they have with their students is to keep them focused on specific educational objectives. Among other things, so the thinking goes, if they
have a clear objective, they will know whether they have met it or not,
and so will those who evaluate them. By the same token, if the day's
SWiBAT is written on the board (as it is supposed to be) then students,
too, can zero in on a specific and attainable goal.

It isn't a crazy thought. Too often in the past, students had no idea
why they were doing a particular assignment, reading a particular
book, or practicing some strange—and to them meaningless—task.
SWiBATs were introduced to get everyone on the same page. But in
addition, SWiBATs supposedly tapped into an important scientific finding from the 1970s, namely, that one of the most powerful ingredients
of intellectual growth is the ability to monitor your own thoughts and
learning: metacognition. When Ann Brown first demonstrated through
her experiments that the ability to notice one's own mental processes
greatly enhanced learning, teachers and principals embraced the idea.
That is why, starting in the early 1980s, you would often hear administrators stopping by a classroom to ask students, "What are you trying
to learn today?" They wanted to make sure that children not only were
learning things but also could explain to others what they were learning. They thought this meant the children were using metacognitive

processes. But being able to tell a grown-up what you are working on is not the same as being aware of what you are learning and why it matters to you.

Whatever the intention, in practice SWiBATs have little to do with metacognition, self-reflection, or any sense of ownership over one's own intellectual processes. They simply turn every lesson into a rush toward a concrete and measurable goal. But Tim's Encoded Story Wall of Time—the crazy name and the funny-looking twelve-foot-tall collage of students' intellectual souvenirs—now, *that* seemed to me like one very exuberant, expressive, but authentic way to get students to think about what kinds of knowledge and skills they were acquiring, and how they were acquiring them.

That first week was a lot of fun. But it wasn't *all* fun. I mentioned that one of the exercises we did was to teach one another things. It was a great exercise and almost everyone was really into it, except for Erik. Erik, or Rix, as everyone called him, came from a family of nonschool people. His older brother had dropped out. He himself, at his best, failed many of his classes or just scraped by. Teachers didn't like him and he didn't like them. At his worst, he cut class or didn't show up to school at all. He admitted, later on, that when he first heard about the Independent Project, he thought it was stupid. Mr. Huron had to convince him to do it, because his options were running out.

The day we taught each other things, he hung back, not engaging. The whole morning he had seemed a bit like a bully in the corner of the playground, with his backward flat-peak cap, his baggy pants, and his ultra-oversized T-shirt, looking on half with disinterest and half with disgust. I couldn't help but feel, at times, like he was sending me a message telepathically: "I've seen this before. These corny exercises. You're wasting my time." And I started to worry that maybe I was.

When everyone else had had their turn, Tim said, "Rix, what about you?" He grunted and stood up, and for the next five minutes he *did* teach us something. But considering we had a day's warning to prepare, it wasn't much. He taught us how to cut paper without scissors—basically an exercise in excessive folding. It seemed like something he thought of at the last minute, right when Tim asked him. Worse, it seemed like a dismissal of the whole exercise: "Look at how meaningless this is." And again, I started to worry that maybe it was. Was I making the same mistakes I was trying to fix?

Within two weeks, Rix showed me just how unnecessary my worry was—a story I'll save for a later chapter. But I bring it up to make it clear that it wasn't all rainbows and butterflies that first week. I had moments of severe self-doubt, bouts of fear, times when my stomach would lurch and I'd think, for the hundredth time, "What am I doing here?"

Still, these moments of anxiety were far outweighed by all the amazing things I saw that first week. I came to school that first day terrified. And I left walking on clouds. I was elated, partly because of some of the stories I've mentioned here, because of some of the things that happened in the beginning that showed me a glimpse of what we might achieve in the coming semester. But mostly it was because we had survived. We had our first day of a student-run school, and we hadn't burned the place down, we hadn't beaten one another up, we didn't even puncture any of the basketballs that took up a good chunk of our one-room schoolhouse. I think that's what a first day is really about.

At the very end of that day, we had a discussion about school up until then, and what we didn't like about it. You can imagine that, with any group of high school kids, if they felt truly free to be honest, that discussion could get a little heated. And it certainly did. At times it was funny. "I mean, it's just so ridiculous that we don't get to have any say over what we learn. We're seventeen years old!" said Mirabelle. She didn't know why that made me laugh so hard and, of course, I couldn't tell her what that teacher had yelled in the CSC meeting— how ridiculous it was to think that seventeen-year-olds could learn on their own.

At times it was unsurprising. There were plenty of the usual complaints. "It's just so frickin' boring." "I feel like half the teachers just don't even like us." "We have so much homework, it takes all night to do it, so they force me to choose between school and the things I love, like filmmaking." At times people shocked me, bringing up things I had never thought of. Dakota said, "I've taken the top English classes all through high school. And in three years I've only read two novels. What the hell's the point?" Mr. Huron chimed in at one point to say, "You know, every day in my office, and down at the garden, I see the potential that exists within these walls. And often, even though no one means to do it, that potential gets squashed." And, at times, it was really upsetting. Dominic, who was slow to open up that first day, finally said, speaking to the floor, his head almost in his lap, "I've just been made to feel stupid for the last couple years. I'm not stupid; I know I'm not. But whenever I walk through those doors, I feel stupid."

Finally, after two hours, the conversation petered out. We had all vented our frustrations with school. And it felt good. We felt purged. We laughed at ourselves a little. "Wow," said Tim, "I just blacked out for the last hour. What did I say?"

Then I told them the real reason for the discussion (other than having a satisfying vent). "Okay," I said. "That's it. We've complained now. But no more complaining this semester. Because there's no one to complain to anymore. Your education is now in your hands. If there's something you don't like, fix it. If you can't fix it on your own, come to the group and ask us to help you fix it. There's no longer anyone who can swoop in to save you, and equally, there's no one else you can lay the blame on if you're not learning. For the next semester, it's all up to us."

The final bell rang, and, amazingly, no one jumped out of their seats. Mr. Huron smiled and said, "That one you should still listen to." Everyone packed their bags and started to shuffle out of the room. We didn't have much time to spare, because the girls' volleyball team and their coach would be moving in any minute. But as we left, Tim turned and put his hand on my shoulder.

"Sam," he said, "this was the best first day of school ever."

When you plan your first day, there are two opposite things to keep in mind: it matters a lot, and it's okay if you mess up. Typically, teachers use the first day to deal with logistics and to clarify expectations and rules. The implicit assumption is that their audience must stay for the whole show, so if things are tedious, or simply procedural at first, it's no big deal. But actually, beginnings are pivotal and will affect the middle and the end.

It's important to set the tone, to make sure students begin the way you hope they'll proceed (active, engaged, interested in one another, in charge of their own education). Ordinarily, this involves students being told what school will be like (what they'll be learning, what the structure of the day will be, what the goals are). In your school, you need to put your money where your mouth is.

At some point every young writer hears the advice, "Show, don't tell." The same is true for your school. Don't tell them what they will experience during the coming term or year. Give them their first taste. Think up activities that bring the core concepts alive. It might not be reading a book or finding the classroom, but whatever it is, it's essential that the students are doing, not being told. In some cases you will want to think of activities that simply turn things on their head. Again, some advice borrowed from writers: make the familiar strange. Help students rethink some things they thought they knew well (like the idea that teachers have all the answers, or that reading is dull). You don't need to cover everything. In fact you don't need to cover anything. You just need to get started.

Which brings us to the second, seemingly opposite point. It's okay if not all of the first day goes well, or if some activity is a flop. To begin with, if nothing else, students will begin to discover that learning is based on making mistakes, not avoiding them. And it's only the beginning. Everyone will have plenty of time to retool, try alternatives, and find their way.

5

ASSUME EVERYONE IS AN INTELLECTUAL

One of the great missteps of high school education has been the idea that only some kids are intellectuals, or want to be. That only some students can grapple with complex ideas, and the others should be given the boiled-down versions of those ideas. That only some kids will be interested in abstractions, and the others should be taught through real-life applications. That only some children will be engaged by things that have no utility in their own lives, and the others need to be taught via contextualization that fits their backgrounds and futures. That only some can love books, or enjoy reading, and the others just need to be taught their ABCs, or how to read a job application.

If you're going to follow this path—to treat only some kids as if they're capable of serious thinking for its own sake—then your school probably isn't worth starting. All students have a right to become better thinkers in school. And all students have the ability to be intellectuals, to thirst for knowledge, to participate in a thoughtful community, to grapple with complex problems. This chapter is about how to act accordingly, and what happens when you do.

Since that first year of the Independent Project I've had a lot of chances to describe it to people. If it's the right audience, I see people nodding enthusiastically. Yeah! Power to the kids! Autonomy! Engagement! Then at some point I get to the part where I say, "So for the next semester, in the mornings, we focused on academics; the natural and

social sciences, English literature and writing, and mathematics." And
I see people's eyebrows bunch up, like, "Huh?" Sometimes, someone
will come up to me afterward and say, "Really cool idea, love it, but . . .
if you had the freedom to let the students do whatever they wanted,
why did you force them to do academics?"

I guess for a lot of people there was a mismatch between the idea
of a school where kids were the authors of their own education and a
school where they still had to do academics. That mismatch never occurred to me. As far as I knew, everyone in high school could think
academically and enjoy academic work. I mean, we didn't all enjoy
memorizing anatomical facts, reading novels we hated, or solving qua-
dratic equations. But we could all think scientifically, enjoy reading
books we chose, and use logic.

At least, that's what I believed going in, and that's why we designed
the Independent Project the way we did. But it's hard to convey properly what it was actually like watching the project unfold over the following months; what it was like watching a group of kids who had
never been treated as intellectuals discover the joy of thinking, the
pleasure of knowledge, and the satisfaction of working hard at things
they were interested in. So here are three stories taken from many that
emerged that semester, which I hope give an idea of what can happen
if you assume everybody is an intellectual.

The first story is about Rix. I mentioned my worries about him in
the previous chapter. By the end of de-orientation week, I was concerned that the Independent Project might have its first failure with
Erik. He had remained relatively disengaged, his chair always pushed
back to the corner of the room, rarely saying anything, answering
questions with grunts. I also mentioned that the Independent Project
was a last resort for him. The deal with Mr. Huron was that he would
try the Independent Project as a way to stick with school, and if that
didn't work, he could always drop out in the spring. That added to the
pressure—if this didn't work, we'd lose him for good.

My fears were only made worse on the first Monday after de-
orientation. Over the weekend, we were all supposed to think about

what our first natural and social science questions would be. Now we were going around the circle, saying what our questions were, and having the group give feedback on the questions (in the beginning most of that feedback came from me, but week by week that grew until most of the feedback came from the rest of the group). Mirabelle said she wanted to ask why we cry.

"Do you mean, what makes people cry?" I asked.

"No," she said, "like, why it evolved."

"Are you asking why it evolved as opposed to other emotional mechanisms that evolve?"

"No, not really. More, like, what use did it have, what benefit did it provide that made it evolve?"

"So it sounds like you're actually asking a 'what' question. For example, what is the evolutionary function of crying?"

We carried on like that around the circle. Dakota was going to see whether there was a pH difference between leaves at the bottom of a nearby mountain and leaves at the top. John wanted to know why Judas betrayed Jesus. Eventually, everyone had gone but Rix. We waited for him to say something, and when he didn't, Tim said, "What about you, Rix?"

"I dunno," he said, the brim of his hat tucked low over his eyes.

"Didn't you think of anything this weekend?" said Mirabelle.

"No," said Rix.

Great, I thought. *This is it. The teachers are right. When the going gets tough, people will just slack off.*

"Come on, Rix," said Tim again. "We all thought of questions. Isn't there anything you're interested in?"

"No," he said, still looking down. "Not really."

A surprising voice spoke up: Dominic. He and Rix were buddies, and he was the last person I would have expected to prod Rix into coming up with a question. I guess I was more small-minded than I realized, and suffered from some of the same handicaps as the teachers I had failed to convince on the CSC. I thought he would have backed his friend in taking the easy route. I was wrong.

His voice as squeaky as ever, Dominic said, "I saw you lookin' at Sam's book earlier."

I racked my brain to think of what book he could possibly be thinking about.

"The one with the stars and shit on the front," said Dominic. And suddenly it clicked. At the time I was reading *A Brief History of Time*, by Stephen Hawking. "You were lookin' at that for ages, man," said Dominic. "Musta thought that was interesting."

There was a long pause. "Yeah, I guess," said Rix. "Infinity and space and stuff. That's kinda cool."

I was hit with a wave of two different emotions at once. First, excitement that Rix said he was interested in something and, second, disappointment that it was something so impossibly complex that he could never make progress on it. For a split second, I considered encouraging him to bite off a smaller chunk. But then I caught myself. The point of this was for people to pursue their interests. I also decided not to push him into coming up with a question. I didn't want to make him decide he wasn't interested after all. "Baby steps," I thought.

But all week long I worried. In the mornings, I'd see people dart off to the library or flip through piles of books. One day I saw Dakota talking animatedly to Mrs. Rawlins, the chemistry teacher, about pH, and the next day I saw her marching into the locker room with muddy boots and a bag full of leaves. John and I had an intense discussion, which occasionally crossed over the line into an argument, about the merit of historical work on religious texts. But every day, I'd see Rix hunched in the corner, in the same spot, looking at the very same page of the same book over and over again. It had a spiral galaxy on the cover.

On Wednesday, I went and sat next to him.

"How's it going?" I asked.

"I dunno," he said. "It's fucking confusing."

"Yeah," I said. "I'm on my second round through *A Brief History of Time* and I still don't get it. You wanna talk about it?"

"Nah, not really," he said.

On Thursday, I couldn't find my copy of *A Brief History*. At lunch, he said, "Yo, I borrowed your book. That cool?"

On Friday, we had our first, exhilarating day of teaching. I watched everyone stand up and teach us about their questions. I had never seen kids look so excited standing in front of a class. Dakota had demonstrations of pH kits, and she had come up with a hypothesis to explain the differences she had discovered in the leaves. John filled three chalkboards with notes about Judas, racing back and forth, trying to fit it all in during his allotted time (we had to fit everyone in on Friday, something I never considered might be a problem but turned out to be a real challenge). Tim told us about the college professor he talked to who had helped him understand how the brain responds to different kinds of drugs to form an addiction.

I watched all of it, happy, excited, fascinated, but all along with a tiny pit of worry about Erik's turn. After everyone else had gone, there was a long pause, and we all turned to look at him. With a kind of embarrassed smile, he said, "I guess I'm s'posed to go now, then, huh?"

He reluctantly stood up, hiked up his pants (which were perpetually falling down), and walked to the front of the room. He tipped his hat down a little, so that we couldn't really see his eyes anymore. Then he reached into his pocket and pulled out a rubber band.

"So I'm gonna show you somethin' called a Möbius strip," he said. And if I thought I was surprised to hear the term "Möbius strip" coming out of Rix's mouth, I only had to wait and listen. "You see," he began, and for the next forty minutes not a single one of us moved a finger. If Rix hadn't been talking, you could have heard us blinking (and we didn't do much of that, either).

He told us about Möbius strips, using the rubber band to demonstrate. He explained how they were useful for understanding curves in space-time. "Because, like, that's what Einstein was saying, was that space and time are kinda one thing, which is hard to understand but makes sense if you look at a picture like this," he said, showing us something in *A Briefer History*, which he must have found in the library, because I didn't own it. He went on to talk a little about the Big

Bang, and finally about the difference between a finite and an infinite universe. "That part's real hard to explain. I tried yesterday to my bro but it didn't work, so maybe this won't make sense, but there's this hotel, and it's, like, an infinite hotel . . ."

I don't know who started it, but when he finished we were all clapping. Erik seemed to lower his hat even further. "Sorry if that didn't make any sense. I still don't get most of it." But underneath his hat he was smiling.

I had heard about Rix weeks and weeks before I met him. In my mind's eye, he was one more nice kid who had somehow been convinced, through life's daily encounters, that he wasn't curious, didn't have academic interests, and couldn't think well. That just infuriated me and pinched my heart. I'm a boy-mom. Even before I realized mine would be a boy family, when I taught elementary school, I felt more comfortable with the boys—even the difficult ones. I loved their energy and their straightforward take on things. So I imagined liking Rix right away and wondered why so many adults had let him down.

Then one day I came to school for a basketball game. I was talking to Sam in the hall, and along came a bony kid with scraggly hair, looking slightly feral. Not appealing at all. The kind of kid who puts adults off, a little neon warning sign blinking on his forehead—"Don't Bother." Sam turned to the boy and smiled, "Hey, Rix. This is my mom. Mom, Rix." This was Rix? The truth is, if I had been his teacher and seen him skulk his way into my classroom, I wouldn't have taken to him at all. I would have assumed he hated me, hated school, didn't want to try, and wasn't going to contribute anything to class. I would have thought the very same things most of his teachers had thought all along.

But here's the kicker. Rix, like all kids, was born an intellectual. Virtually every single person starts life eager to find things out, ready and able to learn, alert to new experiences. Most little kids (barring serious kinds of illness, disability, or trauma) are curious, inventive, interested in testing their hypotheses. In other words, almost all of us begin life with a formidable capacity to learn (even those deemed dull at school are able to learn to talk, navigate their neighborhoods, acquire the vast and subtle rules governing their family life and friendships). But it's not just the capacity to learn that is robust in early childhood. Nearly all young children have a taste for *thinking*. A wide range of studies shows how eager children are to figure out why things work the way they do, what underlies surprises and mysteries. Early in life children are natural scientists, anthropologists, storytellers, mathematicians, and philosophers.

It's true that as we grow up, we naturally lose a little of that open-minded thirst for knowledge—or rather, we trade it in for expertise, focus, and long-term goals. We give up our insatiable need to know everything in return for the ability to navigate everyday life. Maturity tends to tame our natural zest for knowledge. But that just means that as we get older we are slightly less voracious and slightly more cautious in our eagerness for knowledge. It does not mean that our minds shut down, that we lose all of our thirst for knowledge. A two-year-old will tinker with nearly anything; a twelve-year-old will tinker with only some things. A three-year-old asks nearly one hundred questions per hour; a teenager asks questions only when the topic really interests her. Age makes us a bit more picky about feeding our intellectual appetites. However, it is not inevitable that most teenagers will lose interest in having far-ranging discussions, solving problems, or exploring new concepts. That happens only if school teaches a kid that he or she is not capable of deep or careful thinking. School is meant to nurture the life of the mind, not kill it. And if there were ever an age for thinking about life's most intriguing mysteries, it is the age of adolescence. Teenagers long to think abstractly, to tangle with moral dilemmas, to seek various forms of truth, to make and absorb art.

Rix is a perfect example of how this well-worn story unfolds. He probably didn't come across as an intellectual kid. He spoke in unpolished tones. He dressed like a slacker. Perhaps he was rude or didn't pay attention to the teacher when he was young. He might not have grown up among talkers and readers, and maybe others in his family hated school, so he expected to hate school. When students like Rix chafe at the bit or struggle with straightforward (boring) tasks, like vocabulary tests, sheets of math problems, or book reports, they begin to feel they're not academic material, and so do their teachers. They are put in the slow classes. Or teachers give them simpler work, with the understandable notion that it would be better for a boy like Rix to succeed at an easy task than fail at a difficult one.

But this notion, however well intentioned, is based on a common misunderstanding—that kids who are not "academic" are also not intellectual. One of the worst mistakes schools make is to think that just because a kid has trouble learning or doesn't seem academically inclined, he or she isn't drawn to interesting ideas. The vocational and college prep courses are often sucked dry of the very material that might engage teenagers and get their minds going. No matter how much a kid doesn't like school, that kid wants to talk about big ideas: infinity, love, justice, truth. Just listen to their songs and to their conversations when they are not in school. A-plus or F, privileged or impoverished, kids like to use their minds and they like to think about interesting things.

Sam did not carry on his shoulders the burdens of the professional public school teacher. He couldn't have cared less about helping the other students succeed on standardized tests. He didn't have to answer to anyone about whether Rix had "covered" the content specified by the school district or the state. He had only one goal: to get Rix interested enough in an idea or topic that he would have a genuine question about it. Even so, he wavered when he considered urging Rix to try something simpler than Hawking, more accessible than infinity. For that moment, Sam was tempted by the same illusion that sinks so many teachers—that a person can't delve into complex matters until he's learned certain building blocks, that intellectual work is a ladder students must climb up: first they acquire information and preliminary skills, and only then, when they've mastered those basics, can they tangle with big ideas or develop their own. My hunch was that Sam thought Rix would be daunted by difficult material—that it would turn him off. But the mind is not linear. In fact, it's hard to get interested in the kind of content and skills that are found at the bottom of the ladder. Who wouldn't rather think about infinity than learn about the number line? Better to get hooked by infinity and have that become your impetus for learning about the number line than to start with the number line and never want to learn anything more about mathematics.

When Sam told Rix that he didn't get A Brief History of Time either, he shifted both their intellectual worlds, without realizing it. Because in that casual remark he embodied the key to making school a place where everyone becomes a thinker: that you don't need to get it totally. You just need to jump in. Kids like Rix and Sam were schooled to think that the goal of school is to know things. But in reality the goal of school should be to rediscover the pleasures of wading into the unknown.

When Rix explained the Möbius strip to the other students and then admitted he still understood only a little of it, he was, at least for that brief period of time, an intellectual.

The second story is about Mirabelle. I never had to worry about her with the sciences the way I did in the very beginning with Erik. She was, from the get-go, enthusiastic, energetic, open-minded, and eager. Though she came in to the Independent Project thinking of herself as a "non-science" person, her excitement about the program made turning her into a science person a cinch. She picked new questions each week, dove into them headfirst, was quick to seek help within the group, among teachers, and outside the school whenever she needed it, and was always ebullient when teaching us on Fridays.

She wrote in her journal, "It's a shame science was never properly defined for me until my junior year of high school. I had always associated science with test tubes, molecules, tectonic plates, and formulas. . . . [But] science is a method, plain and simple. It's almost impressive that through all my years of schooling no one ever told me that."

She went on to write, "Frankly, I have never enjoyed science class and felt that I never really would. If you had told me that I would fall in love with Stephen Hawking for two weeks I would have laughed in your face." That was referring to the weeks where Erik taught us about space and time. "Setting the preconceived notion aside that I was not good at science and a lot of help from a peer I found myself fascinated. . . . As much as I may want to throw scientific evidence to the side and say 'what do these people know anyway!' I have come to really appreciate how much stronger an argument (no matter if it has to do with art or mirror neurons) is when science is a factor."

It was quick and easy to turn her view of science around. As she points out, all it took was being encouraged to set aside the idea that she was "artsy," not "sciencey," and to work with peers who were excited about it. And the result, on top of becoming better at asking questions and using rigorous methods to get answers, discovering what it was like to be fascinated by what she was learning, and finding dozens of new interests, is that she is now a person who appreciates scientific evidence. If we had achieved nothing else in the Independent Project, I would have been happy with one student learning to appreciate the value of science. And as I said, it was remarkably easy to achieve.

But it was a different story when it came to math. When we switched to the languages halfway through the semester, Mirabelle did an about-face.

"Sam," she said that first day, "I've been super motivated this whole semester. You know I've given my all to the IP, but I just can't do math. I don't want to, either, but even if I did, it wouldn't matter. I am literally incapable."

"Okay," I said, "fine. But before you quit, read the book, and then we can talk again." The book was *Flatland*, by Edwin Abbott Abbott, and it was how we were going to start our work in mathematics. When we switched from the sciences to the languages, it meant we were starting work in the mathematical and English languages. For English, each week someone would choose a novel for the group to read, and on Friday we would have a book discussion, and everyone would read aloud a piece of writing, fiction or nonfiction, they had done in response to the book. But there weren't enough weeks left in the semester for everyone to choose a book, so I opted out and instead chose a math book to read alongside our novel that first week.

Flatland is narrated by a square who lives in a two-dimensional world. The first part of the book explains how a two-dimensional world works. But then the square is visited by a sphere (which appears as a circle that is growing larger as the sphere passes through the plane). The sphere eventually convinces our narrator of a third dimension and then takes him to visit other worlds—a one-dimensional one, a dimensionless one. The climax of the book occurs when the square says to the sphere, "Wow, I wonder what a four-dimensional world is like," and the sphere says, "That's ridiculous, there's no such thing!"

The book is fun and clever, stretches your mind, and, I hoped, was a way to show how mathematical thinking can be used in more exciting ways than plugging numbers into a graphing calculator. Mirabelle read the book and, like everyone else, enjoyed it.

But it didn't convince her to want to do math. "*Flatland* was really cool!" she said. "But it didn't require doing any math . . ."

So I went to my last resort. "Do it for me, then," I said, finally, desperately. "You've loved everything else about the IP. You did amazing things in the sciences; you told me you had fallen in love with learning. Your Individual Endeavor is fantastic. You're loving the novels we're reading. Do this one bit for me, for the Independent Project, just to prove to all the teachers who said we couldn't that we can, that we can do math in the IP."

Well, that worked, sort of. She agreed to keep trying math. But the problem was, she was just doing the same things she had done in traditional school—stuff she hated. The only difference was, rather than being told to do it by a teacher (which hadn't worked), she now had a reason to force herself to do it. She was doing it because she was invested in the school's success, because the school was her own, because she was responsible for it, because she cared about her peers and our rise and fall, and because I had asked her to do it. So she was doing math, yeah, but she wasn't really learning any more about math than she had been before, and she certainly wasn't learning to like or appreciate it.

I see, in those first few weeks, neat writing in Mirabelle's journal about math: "Linear equations: things that continue steadily either positively or negatively. Exponential equations: things that . . . ," and it continues. On another page is a definition for unit circles, and after that a list of symbols (radians, trigonometric functions). You can see she's copying these from a book, or at best reading a sentence, trying to memorize it, and then writing it down. I guess it was good that she was trying. It was a start. But it wasn't good enough.

I realized, at some point, that there was no point pushing on if she wasn't going to be interested. Otherwise I was making the same mistake I was trying to fix. So in a last-ditch effort, I suggested Mirabelle spend the morning trawling through the Internet until she found something math related that interested her. At lunch, she came to me with a printout of a page on biomathematics and elephant movement patterns. Mirabelle loved elephants. I mean, really loved them.

"Well," she said, "if elephants can't get me interested in math, nothing can. So I guess I'll give this a shot."

The change in her journal is so drastic, it's like a different person started writing in it. Now the pages are filled top to bottom, with scribblings all over the place. There are probability-density equations tucked into the corners, with arrows pointing away from symbols, and little notes like "how far away from the origin *something* will be after *this* amount of time," with an arrow linking "*this*" to another symbol, and another arrow from "*something*" that says, "elephants, people, sugar grains in my coffee." Then there are cutouts, articles, photocopies from textbooks, calculations, errors crossed out.

She must have come to me a thousand times in those next couple of weeks with questions. She really struggled with the equations, and any calculations still gave her a lot of anxiety. But the difference was, now she was willing to do whatever it took to try to work them out, because she actually wanted to know the answer, and she actually was excited to be using math to learn about elephants.

Mirabelle will never be a mathematician. She'll never do math in her free time. She says, herself, in an entry in her journal toward the end of the semester, "Now, I suppose it would be a lie to say that I enjoy doing math, but I really have grown to appreciate it and admire those who work in the field. This was a huge leap for me and it was a slow revelation, but I am very glad for it." She goes on to explain what she thinks was different in the Independent Project that finally made her enjoy math. "Naturally we are all curious and interested in things. If we reverse the process and started with those things that we are naturally drawn to, then apply and learn the methods of math that are needed to further explore those subjects [we'd be much better off]." And finally, she writes, "Even if the actual work I did with numbers was not exhilarating, what I was able to discover about predicting randomness in life was very impressive and really convinced me that without math all the things I care about in this world would either not exist, not be able to be explored as thoroughly, or just remain undiscovered."

Sam's last-ditch strategy for luring Mirabelle into math—"Do it for me"—made me cringe a little. Was Sam going to get this pretty girl interested in mathematics by suggesting she do it for him? But then I realized that for as long as I had been in schools, teachers had been telling kids to "do it for them" in one way or another. "Do it because I said so." "Do it because I'll be mad if you don't." "Do it because I'll smile at you if you do." The only difference with Sam and Mirabelle was that, if it worked, she'd be doing it out of friendship. And, I told myself, weren't there times when I had done something not out of fear or the promise of a reward, but because I wanted to connect to someone I admired or liked? Relationships, after all, are among the greatest motivators.

When I was eleven years old, I fell in love with three things all at once: gymnastics, theater, and my teacher. He was my coach and he directed the plays at our school. He had crinkly eyes, crowded, chipped teeth, and a southern accent.

I had never heard anyone speak to students the way that he

did—intense, colorful, and seductive. He told us that people secretly liked the smell of sweat, he quoted Faulkner, and he didn't hesitate to scorch us with an angry glare when we weren't 100 percent focused. All of our other classes and projects had the appeal of mold compared to the exultation we felt working with him. I gravitated toward his intensity as if mesmerized, and he knew that.

One day I was in the gym with him, trying to perfect my back handspring. He kept making me go back to the end of the mat, come running toward him, and just before I got to the end, do a roundoff, the move just before you hurdled yourself backward. I had to do it again and again, because, he insisted, I was on the verge of a breakthrough. As he knelt there at the end of the mat, ready to spot me, he kept shouting, "Again. Again." I must have tried the same move thirty times. I was sick to my stomach with fatigue. I was ecstatic.

Some time ago, Leon Botstein, the president of Bard College, came to the college where I teach to give a talk about how academic institutions should handle sexual relationships between faculty members and students. Many of my colleagues in the audience bristled at what he said. As I recall, he argued that though it was wrong for a professor to have a sexual relationship with a student, it was misguided to try to use the law to prevent such relationships. The thing I remember best was his willingness to say that romance is present when one person is learning from another. He recalled the stories his mother had told him about her girlhood in Switzerland, where she studied piano very seriously with a famous, and famously intense, pianist. She told her son, young Leon, about her piano teacher, "The better I played, the closer he sat."

As psychologists have come to realize, our emotions are deeply bound up with our thoughts, never more so than when it comes to learning. After all, motivation is the key to learning. We've never hesitated to motivate kids with fear of punishment or desire for a prize. Why not motivate them with friendship? Once I overcame my first gut reaction and thought it over, "Do it for me" started to seem like a really good idea.

But meanwhile, I had another nagging doubt about Mirabelle. Watching her over the years, I got the feeling that she liked the idea of being one of the thoughtful literary kids more than she liked actually pursuing a thought or mastering a new body of information. She liked thinking about big ideas from a distance, without having to get into the nitty-gritty of working on an idea herself, or conducting a painstaking piece of research. If she loved something, she dove in willingly. But if a topic seemed difficult to her, she circled around it, giving it a wide berth.

Like most kids in our culture, Mirabelle was brought up to believe that there were things she was naturally good at (reading and art) and things that she wasn't good at (science and math). Watching her thread her way through school, I saw her use a familiar strategy for topics that scared or bored her: she kept them at arm's length, doing what she needed to in order to get reasonable grades, but avoiding any real contact with the ideas, intellectual procedures, or experiences she might need to get a feel for the discipline. This way of taking a class is sort of like eating something you know is good for you but tastes bad. You try to swallow it without smelling it, and you certainly don't let it linger on your tongue. And just as the person who eats vegetables as if they are medicine will never become someone who loves healthy food, the student who treats complex or challenging topics as if they were porcupines will never really get anything out of what they are studying. And yet, it's a common strategy, especially among students like Mirabelle who want to think of themselves as "good" students. The sad part is, the curriculum supports such a tentative and disengaged approach.

It's not reasonable to expect teenagers to love every subject. After all, we don't require adults to. Yet students have few options for dealing with a course in which they have no interest. The first, very popular option is to turn their backs on a topic that seems hard or boring. They tell themselves they aren't good at it, they don't care about it, it has no meaning in their lives. Kids often accept the fact that they'll fail or just skate by.

The second option is to figure out how to game the system. Many kids are savvy enough to do just enough of the homework to get an okay grade. They learn whatever procedures allow them to answer the questions (skim the paragraph in order to summarize it, memorize the science they need for the lab report, or learn the steps for conducting a statistical test). Alternatively, they may simply figure out some good test-taking strategies. Adam Gopnik, writing about taking the test for his learner's permit as an adult, shares the advice his son Luke gave him: Skip the two answers that are obviously wrong and choose between the two plausible ones. Gopnik then zeroes in on the meaning of such a strategy: "The American social truth—that what we spend years teaching our children is essentially to spot the two obviously wrong answers."

Lots of kids want to do okay in school without having to learn material they don't like. These kids simply follow some version of Luke's advice to his dad.

Finally, there are the kids who work hard in a class they don't really like, just to get a good grade. But just because a student does well in a class does not mean he has learned anything significant or useful.

It seemed to me that a kid like Mirabelle could avoid math, with greater or lesser adroitness, as students have done for decades. Or she could give it a real go. She might not become a math convert. Why should she? But at least she could tangle with it in a deeper, more authentic way than was her custom. Rather than skimming the surface of mathematics to attain the veneer of competence, what Mirabelle needed was to tackle a smaller piece of the discipline and get into the guts of it.

It may seem like a slight achievement: Mirabelle came to appreciate people who do math. But what she gained is more potent than you might think. Her mind won't shut down the minute people begin to talk about math. Her eyes won't glaze over the minute she encounters a statistic or graph in a newspaper. She's likely to approach the world of numbers in a different way. She finished the IP with something all her previous required math courses had not given her: a feel for what it's like to view the world through a mathematical lens, and a sense of what it takes to think in mathematical terms. She went from cautious bystander to comfortable novice.

No small feat, and much more powerful than a bunch of procedures she's eager to forget as soon as she can. And all of that in only eight weeks. Imagine if her work on random walks had been only the first step. Imagine if she had had a full year, or four full years, learning math by getting inside of it. Who knows how far she would have gone?

One last story. I mentioned Dominic earlier, and that he was severely dyslexic and failed many of his classes. He came to the Independent Project never having read a novel, at least not in school. So the fact that we were going to be reading a novel every week, unsurprisingly, totally freaked him out.

"I won't be able to keep up with you guys," he said grumpily that first day of the languages. Fine, we all told him. We didn't care, as long as he just read what he could and talked about whatever he had read in our discussions on Fridays.

I had no idea what books we would be reading, because a different person chose each week. Tim went first and chose *The House on Mango Street*, by Sandra Cisneros, a coming-of-age novel about a Mexican American girl. It's a book that's read by adults but also targeted to young adults, so it's an easy read; perhaps Tim chose it because he was an Asian American son of a first-generation immigrant.

"Yo, I can't do this," said Dominic angrily on Tuesday, throwing the book down.

"Come on, Dominic," said Tim. "I chose this book because I wanted all of you to read it. Don't bail on me, man."

"I feel stupid trying to read it. I feel like I did in regular school again." This was halfway through the Independent Project, and during the sciences—like Mirabelle—Dominic had really come into his own, saying that he liked school for the first time in his life.

"None of us care if you finish it, Dominic," said Mirabelle. "It doesn't matter. We all have strengths and weaknesses. Look at how useless I am at math."

But on Friday, Dominic refused to read aloud the piece of writing he did. He agreed to give it to me and Mr. Huron, as long as we didn't show it to anyone else. It was only about a paragraph long, and simply described what had happened in the first couple of chapters of the book.

The next week it was John's turn to choose. I expected something really difficult from him. He was the most literary of all of us and at the time was reading *War and Peace* for pleasure. But he surprised me by choosing *Charlotte's Web*. He later explained to us that he thought E.B. White was America's greatest author, and he gave a few of us some of his essays to read as well. But at the time, I was just happy that we had another easy book for Dominic to read.

"Fuck this, I'm watching the movie," Dominic said on Wednesday. "I'm never gonna finish this by Friday."

Week by week, it seemed, Dominic made it a little further before tossing the book aside angrily. Every Friday he refused to read aloud from his writing. And every Friday he seemed a little surprised that we weren't mad that he hadn't finished the book. When I was younger, I used to annoy the hell out of my older brother. It was essentially my purpose in life. So he'd rough me around—throw me off the couch, put me in a headlock, give me a dead arm—and it usually worked, at least in the short term, for getting me to stop. Sometimes, though, I'd do something by accident that I thought might annoy him, like knock over his glass of water. He'd reach out to pick up the water glass and, out of instinct, I'd duck and cower.

Dominic was a bit like that on Fridays. "I didn't finish the book," he'd say defiantly, and then brace himself as though expecting us to lash out. "Okay," we'd say, "fine. Just talk about what you read." Or, "Whatever, your loss, we're about to spoil the end for you."

Eventually we came to Dominic's week for choosing a book. "You guys are gonna think it's stupid," he said.

"Dominic," said John, "you gave all of our books a shot. We'll give your book a shot too, even if it is stupid."

"It's got pictures in it," said Dominic, still sounding like he was waiting for us to turn on him.

The book was *Tales of the Weirrd* by Ralph Steadman, a British cartoonist. It certainly was strange, and it wasn't a novel—it was a collection of stories, with illustrations, about extremely eccentric people from the nineteenth century. But we all read it, and we all found it hugely entertaining. "How 'bout the guy who started to grow the beard at age four?" "What about the blind caricaturist? That was so cool!"

Dominic seemed transfixed by all of us talking and debating excitedly over the book he had chosen. On Friday he was laughing, listening, explaining, adding more backstory to the book. He had spent sixteen years unable to keep up with others as they zoomed along through their books, unable to join in or contribute, marginalized and made to feel like an outsider to reading. Now everyone was reading *his* book, everyone was asking *him* questions about it, and everyone was grateful to *him* for having chosen such a cool thing for us to read.

The following week was Dakota's turn to choose a book. She was definitely the brainiest of the group. So I wasn't surprised when she chose *As I Lay Dying*, by William Faulkner. Well, I thought, if Dominic hadn't finished *Charlotte's Web*, he wouldn't make it three pages into Faulkner.

He read it cover to cover. He told us on Friday, a little embarrassed but also I think happy, that he had had to read every day before and after soccer practice to get it done. But he said he identified with Darl. And, in fact, he had written an alternate ending from Darl's perspective in jail. He still wouldn't read it aloud to us. But he said it was okay if Mirabelle read it for him.

I can easily imagine Dominic's experience in first grade. I've seen so many kids, especially boys, hang their heads lower and lower as the rest of the group learns to read. They're mortified that they can't do what comes so easily to the others. They begin to dread reading time. The more they dread it, the more they hold books, and reading, at arm's length. But it's not just the reading itself that becomes such a source of gloominess. It's the sense that they're not part of the group. If that's tough when you're six or seven, imagine how excruciating it is when you're fifteen or sixteen. In our culture, if you can't read easily, you might as well wear a dunce cap around school. No wonder Dominic didn't want to read. And the more he didn't want to read, the less reading experience he got. By high school he still hadn't become a skilled reader. He had missed out on all the stories, characters, plot twists, and ideas that other kids had access to. His inner landscape was constrained by what he hadn't read, and his social landscape was therefore limited too. Dominic's intellectual experience had been defined by his limitations. Now, for the first time, it could be defined by his interests.

The question educators ask themselves all the time is, "How late is too late?" Can a sixteen-year-old become interested in books if he doesn't read easily? No teenage boy is going to willingly work on reading skills. It's dreary and humiliating and feels pointless. But, given a chance to be part of a book discussion, a boy like Dominic might tackle it from the opposite direction. He might begin with the ideas and stories, and with the chance to share those experiences with friends, he might also get better at reading.

When I was in high school and college, I could tell you, on any given day, what the other people in my family were reading. If I didn't know, I felt strange—like not knowing whether they had a pet or not, or whether they had been sick. When I met a new friend, or dated someone, the acid test was finding out what books they liked. For me, this was as important a step in becoming close as telling someone about my childhood.

The most important thing people get out of college is not preparation for a particular kind of job. Instead, at its best, college gives students a sense of intellectual community. Eating together in the dining halls and talking after class gives students the feeling that they share a frame of reference—one rooted, at least partially, in the world of books, research, and ideas. But it's not only that. College gives students the habit of backing up opinions with evidence, offering reasons, asking questions in order to learn more, and using written material to learn about things beyond one's immediate experience. In other words, far beyond specific technical skills, the value of college comes from the intellectual habits it instills.

By choosing books *for* one another, revealing to their classmates their favorite stories, becoming closer friends through reading, the kids in the Independent Project had created their own reading club. What teenager wouldn't find a book club of his peers more engaging than a class in which a teacher assigned a book and decided what aspects of the book to discuss? Turning reading into a social experience in high school is a great way to get lots more students interested in books. But it may also pave the way for a lifelong interest in sharing ideas with others—in creating an intellectual community. When a kid chooses a book for her peers to read, she puts herself on the line. She *wants* the others to see what she saw in it. When a kid reads a book his classmate loves, he learns something new about her; and because of her, he can see something important and new in the book. It's true that the most avid readers can happily read book after book all by themselves, without ever talking to anyone about it. One of the glories of reading is that it can be so solitary. But few adolescents are that solitary, and the ones who already read that way don't need to do it in school. Kids like Dominic need to read and think with others. And here I don't mean in a room with others, or simply reading the same book as others. I mean communing over books.

Here we come to another barrier the group in the Independent Project happily crashed their way through: the barrier of ability groups. The most literary kid in the group, Dakota, assigned one of the great works of American fiction. The least literary kid in the group, Dominic, was perhaps the most profoundly affected by it. The idea that you should talk only to those who are just like you is such a bad idea it's strange we ever think it has a place in school. Quite the opposite. Dakota learned something new about a favorite book. Dominic learned something new about fiction. And neither could have learned what they did without the other.

When Dominic sunk his teeth into *As I Lay Dying*, he finally knew what it felt like to be a reader, to have a book really speak to him. And that, of all things, is the most potent and enduring accomplishment of high school.

"Intellectual" is one of those words, like "curiosity" or "creativity," that is easy to embrace in name only. Nearly all teachers and school administrators, and most parents, too, agree that it's great to be curious, that kids should love learning, that creativity is valuable. If you ask principals whether they think it's important for students to learn how to think, not one of them will scoff and answer, "Don't be silly. They're not here to think, just to follow rules." Most educators believe they fully endorse the value of creative, rigorous thinking, and many educators believe that's what they're helping their students reach for (though there are still some who are convinced the purpose of school is to memorize facts).

But if you go into a school and look for signs that all the teenagers, not just the ones headed to good colleges, are tangling with complex, interesting problems, you'll be hard-pressed to find what you're looking for.

It's not enough to say that you're going to assume everyone is an intellectual. Paying lip service to a certain attitude or point of view is a long way from putting it into action. So how do you make your school a place where everyone is treated as a thinker?

Make sure there is a wide range of students with a wide range of interests. Find a way to make them responsible for sharing their interests, areas of expertise, and thinking methods with one another. Hitch them to one another's ideas by having them assign books, critique one another's research, explain why they each love what they love. Ensure that they become intellectually close to one another by designing the day in such a way that students depend on one another for the material they use, the questions they ask, the responses they construct, and the reasons they give. Make their ideas interdependent.

Make sure at least one person in the group really feels comfortable asking questions, modeling ignorance, and improvising in the pursuit of knowledge. Keep intellectual topics at the center of the day and don't confuse intellectual with academic. Make time for serious discussion, and hold everyone to that, until it becomes a habit.

*Encourage a wide variety of materials—*Charlotte's Web, Many Moons, As I Lay Dying. *It ensures that there are ways for every single student to stretch in a new direction, and it creates a plurality of perspectives—the key to deep thinking.*

And finally, don't confuse "student run" with "nonacademic," or "creativity and engagement" with "unintellectual." There is no dichotomy between self-directed learning and intellectual rigor. At their best, they are one and the same.

6

REQUIRE MASTERY

So far, we have identified certain kinds of intellectual work that we think are essential: asking and improving questions, reading novels, sharing knowledge with others. We have also stressed how important it is for every student to figure out some questions that they really care about delving into. But none of these will amount to much unless the students attain depth of knowledge and advanced skill in a domain. One of the most potent things a student can experience in high school is the chance to get better and better at something, know more and more about it, until he is something of an expert in that field. Everyone should master at least one discipline: a complex and significant body of knowledge that entails a specific set of skills and results in work (artistic, intellectual, or practical) that is useful and meaningful to others. Step six is the simplest one to take, the most difficult one to take fully, and the most important one to execute well. But we hope that this chapter will make it easier to do just that.

When I was thirteen, in eighth grade, I had a problem. I had completed all the math and Spanish classes at the middle school, so I needed to take some courses up at the high school. There were various complications. The walk from the middle school to the high school took about ten minutes and required crossing a main road, walking through the grounds of the elementary school, and climbing a small hill. The schedules of the two schools were not aligned, so I couldn't just go up to the high school during middle school math and languages time. And the periods at the two schools were different lengths, meaning that when I came back down to the middle school after my high school classes, I'd have to wait around for an hour and a half for my next class to start. Fortunately, everyone seemed fine with me making the long journey on my own, unmonitored. It turned out that despite the misalignment between the schedules, I'd only be missing my electives, like music and art, and everyone at the school was happy with that too.

It was the last issue—the hour and a half of unstructured time at the middle school—that threw everyone into a tizzy. "An hour and a half?! What the hell's the boy going to *do* all that time? Do we even have a procedure for dealing with something like this? *Is it even feasible?*" At least, that's what I imagined the middle school administration saying. I don't really remember the details. There was a lot of hand-wringing about how I might spend that time, and everyone was worried. Except me. I thought it was great. I could do whatever I wanted! Sky's the limit. I asked them if I could spend the time working on a project, and they said sure, skeptically.

I decided I wanted to spend the year studying a pond.

Every Monday after school I walked through the woods to a large pond near my house that had been split in two by a beaver dam. The pond wasn't on my parents' land, and the very first Monday I was there, I heard crunching in the leaves behind me. I turned around to find the man who owned the property. He didn't live there, but he had a hunting cabin in the woods. He had a golden retriever at his side and a shotgun in his hand. He told me I was lucky I didn't get shot (though perhaps what he meant was, *he* was lucky I didn't get shot). He said if I planned to be wandering around in his woods, I better get permission first.

So every Sunday night, I rang his house and asked him if I could visit the pond the following day between 3 and 5 p.m. That first Monday in September I spent forty minutes down at the pond. I didn't see much. By June, I was spending several hours there and could fill pages of my journal with everything I saw.

During the week, in my free time at the middle school, I researched any new plants or animals I had seen and wrote up what I learned along with any relevant observations I had made. By the end of the year, I had a two-hundred-page manuscript—a natural history of the pond. But more important, it was the first time I had a taste of what it was like to master something. I knew that pond better than anyone else in the world. I had become an expert on the comings and goings of its flora and fauna. I knew more about the species found there than I knew about anything else. And above all, I had fallen deeply, truly in love with something that wasn't a person.

When I had finished the manuscript, I sent it to my hero, an evolutionary biologist and entomologist named E.O. Wilson. I never expected a reply. But I got one. He sent a note and said he enjoyed my book. And then he said, "First your magic pond, then the world."

"My magic pond," I remember thinking. "*My* pond."

What I got a taste of with the pond, I feasted on with Project Sprout. As the garden grew, so did my attachment to and investment in it. My freshman year I was captain of the JV basketball team and played shortstop for the baseball team. By junior year, I had quit both for the garden. I missed family trips, science fairs, and parties. In four years of high school, I never slept past seven on a Saturday morning in the fall or spring, because that was when we had community volunteer days. And every year, the spring started earlier and the fall ran later. Of all the thousands of photos that were taken at Project Sprout, my very favorite one is a photo of seven of us Sprouters, thigh deep in two feet of snow, pruning raspberries.

I learned what it was like to become completely devoted to something. To learn everything I could possibly learn about it. To give every minute of my free time to it. Once again I had fallen in love with something that wasn't a person or an animal, but an *endeavor*.

Along the way, I learned how to plan an event for hundreds of people, lead a team, organize a workforce, and inspire people for a cause. I learned how to build a greenhouse, deliver a speech to ten thousand people, roast a pig, and grow vegetables by the ton. I learned about working with my peers, working with my non-peers, teaching little kids, having my colleagues turn on me, building something from the ground up, and learning to give away something that was my life for four years; and, most important, I experienced failure after failure after failure.

I became aware of all these benefits only much later, when I was in college. I never thought at the time, "Wow, I gained a lot from the pond study and Project Sprout; other people should learn those skills as well." I just thought, "Wow, this feels good." And I wanted all of my friends to experience that feeling too.

That's why mastery, in the form of the Individual Endeavor, was a central part of the Independent Project day. I had seen people in school flitting about from subject to subject, always skimming the surface, never learning what it was like to really take hold of something and make it their own. And that didn't seem fair. It seemed to me that everyone in school should have the opportunity to master something. Everyone should find their magic pond.

From the time I was twelve until I was nineteen, I spent my summers running a camp for little kids. At first it was your garden-variety summer camp—I took the children swimming and they painted and made collages, acted out plays, sang songs, and ate lots of snacks. I didn't even drive, so my mom had to help when I wanted to take my little campers on a field trip.

I loved everything about my summer camp—preparing for the kids' arrival, figuring out how to talk to the parents, making the kids' snacks, and coming up with cool activities. But after the first few years, it seemed a little flat, just a string of nice pastimes. Even then, I had some inchoate intuition that my little campers were being only half tapped. And it bothered me. I thought about it during the summer, and I thought about it in the long months that followed.

Sometime during the winter before the third year of the camp, I had a mini-revelation. I realized that the best part of my own school year was the plays we performed. I loved acting, but I also loved the long rehearsals, the intense pressure of having to get the costumes and set ready, the eleventh-hour crises when one of the actors got sick and the understudy had to take over. It seemed to me, even as a fifteen-year-old, that working together on those plays brought out the best in all of us. It dawned on me that my little campers might love the same thing, which was why the very next summer, my camp became a children's theater.

Even now, in my late fifties, that funny little children's theater stands out as one of the best things I've ever done. During those teenage summers my camp completely absorbed me. In early spring I'd begin planning for the coming season—designing a mailing, finding ways to advertise, and looking for space I could rent. Once summer began, I'd get up at 6 a.m. and begin preparing, so that everything would be ready when the children arrived. Long after they had gone home each afternoon, I would think of new activities, arrange field trips, prepare projects, and buy supplies. I loved it, I was good at it, I wanted it to succeed, and I would do anything to make it better.

Years later, when my first son, Jake, was miserable in middle school, I began to think back to those thrillingly arduous and absorbing summers. They saved my adolescence. And it dawned on me that Jake, too, needed something that would soak up all of the simmering frustrations, yearnings, and mental unrest of adolescence. In his case, it was sculpture. He began working with an artist who lived nearby, helping in her studio once a week. For his brother Will, on the other hand, 85 percent of his teenage years was spent spilling his blood and guts onto a basketball court or baseball diamond. And in Sam's case, the garden was his life.

More and more research shows that teenagers who spend time each week completely consumed in some challenging activity are the ones most likely to thrive over the long haul. And though some of the subjects described in these studies match the iconic image of the talented teen devoted to cello or the school newspaper, some are, instead, completely obsessed with car repair or orienteering.

Teenagers crave mastery. And why wouldn't they? Mastery feels good, and so do the steps required to attain mastery. Standing on the cusp of adulthood, what would lure a teenager forward? Autonomy, sure, but just as compelling, a sense of competence and self-assurance. In other words, expertise. What does it take to become a young adult eager to gain expertise?

Fifteen years ago, if you'd walked into any faculty lounge, you'd hear the most devoted and compassionate teachers talking about their students' self-esteem. Parents and educators had been convinced (primarily by psychologists) that children could do well only if they felt good about themselves. A struggling child was a child with low self-esteem, and a thriving child, so the conventional wisdom went, was one who probably had a robust sense of her own self-worth. It's no exaggeration to say that during those years teachers talked about self-esteem as if it were a bodily substance that could be measured, like a person's temperature or BMI. I heard teachers say things like, "Well, his self-esteem is way down. We've got to get it higher," and, "She has good self-esteem. She got that in fourth grade." I always imagined the mercury rising and falling on the esteem-o-meter.

But then there was a backlash. Psychologists began to discover that praising kids all the time is not the best way to improve a kid's sense of self (and often has unintended negative consequences). Don't misunderstand. Having confidence and liking oneself are undoubtedly important. We know from decades of research that uncertainty, timidity, and tentativeness often prevent learning and lead to failure. But children don't become confident or determined by hearing a lot of praise. They get those qualities by doing well at difficult tasks, accomplishing goals they've set for themselves, mastering skills, and seeing meaningful fruits of their labor. Teenagers, bullshit detectors that they are, know the difference between being told they've done a good job and actually doing a good job.

Angela Duckworth has shown that grit—the ability to persevere, stay focused, and delay gratification—rather than praise is essential to academic success. Her studies show that in fact grit is a better predictor of high school grades than intellectual capacity. Teachers (and parents) have taken this and run with it. Kids need to focus; they need to try hard and then harder; they need to settle in for the long grind.

But this love affair with self-control, effort, and hard work begs the question: grit for what? As psychologist Marlene Sandstrom says, grit without passion becomes grout. And yet the opposite is just as problematic. A general sense of excitement about learning and a "feel" for various topics will get a student nowhere if he or she doesn't know how to dive in and toil.

The experience of a student of mine at Williams College, named Manuel, captured this perfectly. He told me that his parents, who were born in Mexico, left school in the sixth grade and immigrated to the United States when they were young adults. His mother had been paralyzed from the waist down as a young woman. Manuel grew up in a trailer park in Texas, along with his two brothers. His father did maintenance at the high school he attended. His life, in other words, had been extremely tough, and his family had faced one kind of obstacle after another. When Manuel described his life story to me, sitting there in the bucolic and privileged campus coffee shop in Williamstown, a student at one of the most demanding and elite colleges in the country, I was stupefied. How, I asked him, had he found his way to Williams from that background? He said, "I had a lot of determination. My parents worked hard, and I knew I'd have to work hard, too, to achieve anything." I told him that I, too, thought effort mattered, but I was worried that the national preoccupation with grit was steering everyone toward an even grimmer (and futile) approach to education. He smiled. "Of course," he said. "I was hell-bent on becoming an immigration lawyer. For me, all the difficulty I faced getting here was worth it because of where I was headed. It's not enough to be determined, to sweat. You have to have something in mind."

When I think back to my summer theater program, Small Potatoes, what made it such a pivotal experience was not simply that I found it absorbing—movies, dancing, and boys were also absorbing. It was that Small Potatoes offered me a really engrossing set of complex challenges—something I could become a master of by working hard, by throwing myself into it, and by thinking about it all the time.

Students in the IP were supposed to develop an initial idea for their Individual Endeavor over the summer. We then spent the week of de-orientation talking to others, getting feedback, investigating possibilities, and finally helping each student to settle on an endeavor. For some people, this came easily and naturally. These were the kids who already knew what they cared about and perhaps had experience pursuing hobbies and interests in a serious way outside of school.

Tim had always loved making short skateboarding and music videos. He had also always loved making beats on his computer. So he said he was going to write, direct, and produce a short film, and write and produce a score for it as well. It seemed perfect. It was ambitious, required a diversity of work, and could easily take a semester to complete. Mirabelle, who was passionate about fighting domestic abuse and rape, decided to write, produce, and air a podcast series on rape, with the goal of raising awareness and helping victims find support. Again, it seemed ideal. She'd have to write, interview people, do research, learn how to get radio time, learn how to edit a podcast, and all of it related to something that was really meaningful. From jump street I could see how endeavors like these could be extremely successful and transformative.

But that wasn't the case for everyone. Dominic couldn't think of anything. He was a curious guy, easily taken with odd and kooky momentary interests—a day of worshiping Tesla, a day of learning how to cobble shoes, a day of collecting artifacts on the railroad tracks—but he had never experienced pursuing a single thing for an extended period of time. During de-orientation week, every hour he seemed to flip-flop between different ideas for an endeavor. "I'm gonna build a boat," he'd say at lunch. And then at 2 p.m. he'd say, "Nah, I could never do that in a semester. I'm gonna hike all the trails around my house." And at the end of most days, he'd say, "Forget it, there's just nothing I'm that interested in."

I remember every time he said that, because each time I'd get this niggling fear that the teachers in the CSC meetings had been right. "What about the kids who just don't have any interests?" they had said, and I had countered ferociously that every kid *could* become interested in something, if given the chance. But each time Dominic said, "I dunno, man, there's just nothin' I wanna do for a whole semester," I'd think, "Maybe I was wrong."

On Friday afternoon of de-orientation week, he said, "I'm gonna learn how to play the piano. I've always wanted to learn an instrument, so now's the time. " Well, at least he had settled on something. Playing the piano fit the requirements for an Individual Endeavor. Dominic wanted to do it, and it could take a whole semester.

But every day after lunch he'd disappear. At a certain point, I started to worry. This was someone who had been seriously considering dropping out before joining the Independent Project. Maybe he was just going home every day and smoking a joint and playing video games. So I would occasionally ask him, as casually as I could, if I could hear him play. "Nah, man," he'd say, avoiding my eyes, "not good enough yet." And so my worries grew. A couple of times I went to the band room to see if he was playing the piano there, and he wasn't. Eventually, thinking that this might have become a serious issue, I brought it up with Tim. Tim knew Dominic better than I did, and I thought he might have an idea what Dominic was up to.

"Well, I'll say this," said Tim. "If he is fucking around, it's not in any obvious place. I'm all over the school getting footage for the film, and I've never seen him in the afternoons either."

So one day I set out to look for him properly. I wandered the whole school, checking empty classrooms, the auditorium, the band room (again), and the cafeteria—all with no luck. I was just starting to think that he really was going home in the afternoons, which I'd have to address with him, when I heard a very faint noise that sounded like it might be a piano. I followed it and came upon the long-forgotten music storage room, the one that had once been suggested as a home for the IP.

I crept up to the door and poked my head in. There, in the corner of the room, his back to me, sitting at an old wooden piano, was Dominic. It would be a stretch to say he was *playing* the piano. He was hammering out the same chord progression, over and over again, and every time he messed up, he'd start over. Occasionally I'd hear him grunt, "Fuck," and once or twice he hit the keys.

I stood there, feeling a little guilty for what amounted to spying on him, but also completely transfixed, for maybe fifteen minutes. He must have played the same sounds a thousand times. He never wavered, turned from the keyboard, or checked his phone. This was someone whose teachers thought he had ADHD, and yet here he was, with a degree of focus and persistence I've seen on only a few occasions, in anyone.

For the next few weeks, I would swing by the music storage room and watch Dominic. I never told him that I had found his hiding spot, and at times I felt guilty. But it was so amazing to watch him I couldn't help myself. He was in there every afternoon, banging away at the keys, learning to read music, trying over and over and over again. And bit by bit, he got better.

Eventually I stopped watching. After all, Dominic deserved better than to be checked up on. Occasionally, after that, I would ask him if I could hear him play, and he'd always have the same answer. "Not good enough." I suspected that maybe he would never be particularly good at piano. But that didn't matter. He was learning what it was like to devote himself to something day in and day out, to try to master it.

At the end of the semester, everyone had to do a presentation of some kind (it could take any format) to demonstrate what they had achieved with their Individual Endeavor. The presentations would be public; one during the day, with the whole school invited, and one at night, with parents and members of the community invited. Dominic was going to do a jazz performance.

I hadn't heard him play since I stopped standing by the doorway to the music storage room. Now I sat in the audience, surrounded by people, with Dominic sitting at a piano onstage, wearing his usual baggy clothes and flat-peak cap. I found myself growing more and more nervous. What if he couldn't do it, and he felt like his endeavor was a failure?

But then he started, and for the next twenty minutes the auditorium was filled with beautiful jazz piano. He read the sheets; he played; he improvised. No one moved an inch, except for the occasionally irresistible applause at a particularly impressive set. At the end, there was a standing ovation, and Dominic's face lit up in a big smile. "Give a bow!" yelled Tim, clapping ferociously, and Dominic did, looking embarrassed and proud.

I remembered something Dominic had said a few weeks before. We had all been talking about whether the Independent Project would survive; whether the School Committee would approve the pilot and give it permanent status. Dominic had suddenly piped up and said, "This isn't a pilot for me. This is real school. This is actual learning." I found myself thinking, "You're right, Dominic. And this is real jazz. This is actual music." And I found myself hoping that this wasn't the last time I heard Dominic play the piano.

Dominic went on to start a jazz band.

Sam comes from a long line of school lovers. When I was little, my mother helped start a K–12 school in eastern Long Island. Having left New York City and her job as a social worker to live with my stepfather on his farm in Sagaponack, New York, my mother found herself looking for a new vocation. She had come across two books that set her on a new path: How Children Fail, by John Holt, and 36 Children, by Herb Kohl. Both books brought to life the excitement and possibility of progressive education—taking fear out of the classroom, replacing dull tasks with interesting work, and giving children a lot more freedom. My mother and her new friends in Long Island set out to build a school based on the ideas she found in those books. So, at age seven, I left the one-room schoolhouse I had been attending to come to this exciting new school. It opened its doors in September 1968, with thirty-five children and seven teachers. It was bursting with life. I have vivid memories of that year: fourteen-year-old Tina Cato getting sent home for wearing a miniskirt with an American flag sewn across her butt; reading *D'Aulaires' Book of Greek Myths* and coming to our festival as Aphrodite, for which I wore my mother's white satin nightgown and a blond hairpiece; learning what the word "observation" meant in science; and planning a fair to raise money for the next year.

In the years that followed, the school embodied the core tenets of progressive education: learning how to learn was more important than mastering particular content, not all students had to learn the same thing at the same time, and teachers should teach what they loved most. This last came in part from an idea that Jerome Bruner vividly put forth in his classic book *The Process of Education*, written in 1960. He argued that any child could learn any subject at any age, so long as it was taught in a way that fit the child's developmental level. And here is where progressive schools, like the one I attended, went astray. In their admirable attempt to make good on the ideas of thinkers like Bruner, Kohl, and Holt, teachers came to think that any topic was as good as any other, as long as the teacher and students were really excited about it. If learning how to learn mattered more than memorizing specific subject matter, the implicit logic went, students could learn critical thinking, how to apply what they knew well to new situations, and how to put information together across disciplines within any number of topics. Instead of a set list of essential books, specified facts in history, or particular topics in mathematics, kids could learn how to think while studying things they loved.

It was a great idea. However, for reasons that are somewhat mysterious, perhaps having to do with other aspects of the 1960s, the idea played out in a slightly strange way. For instance, I took a course one year in witchcraft. Another year I did all my social studies reports on costumes around the world. Somehow, unwittingly, schools like the one I attended had made an unfortunate trade—enthusiasm and liveliness replaced breadth and significance. Often what kids studied was quirky at best, and irrelevant at worst. In one renowned progressive school in Manhattan, it seemed that several cohorts of students studied monarch butterflies for six years in a row because so many teachers had decided that butterflies were the passion they wanted to share with their class.

During the weeks that Sam skulked worriedly outside the room, eavesdropping on Dominic practicing the piano, I secretly wondered whether jazz counted as a worthwhile pursuit. Would Dominic learn things that extended beyond the piano? Should the kids in the Independent Project be free to take on any kind of Individual Endeavor?

When Ted Sizer published his groundbreaking trilogy about public education (beginning with *Horace's Compromise*), in the 1990s, he suggested that before graduating, every student should have to demonstrate expertise in something. Those performances, as they came to be known, embodied the same principle we are talking about here— that depth is more important than breadth, and that genuine rigor comes from knowing something well, rather than knowing lots of things superficially.

But just as learning how to learn took a misstep in the 1960s, so, too, Sizer's demonstrations got watered down. In many schools that joined Sizer's Coalition of Essential Schools, kids ended up choosing strangely narrow and often superficial topics for their demonstrations: how to ride an ATV in the snow, how to build a bluebird house, the science of taste buds. Basically the original concept, which was to push kids toward mastery of something they cared about, became just another project—in many schools it became one more item to check off the list of requirements. Often students set themselves tasks or chose topics that were neither complex nor challenging, but instead merely seemed manageable in a busy schedule. Having embraced the nine principles of the coalition, schools nevertheless allotted far too little time for the students to tackle their projects in any real depth or to achieve true expertise. Then, because students ended up tacking on these projects as an afterthought in senior year, squishing them in with all the other "serious" requirements, it wasn't fair to evaluate them in the rigorous way Sizer had in mind. So it was not surprising that schools ended up providing somewhat perfunctory and meaningless feedback. It became just another rite of passage to tick off as long as the student didn't bungle it completely.

But the failures of those efforts did not undermine Sizer's concept, as some skeptics claimed. Expecting students to master something and demonstrate their mastery was a great idea. It just was harder than you might think to export into schools mired in a very different set of traditions and educational customs. I once heard someone say to Sizer, "But so many of the coalition schools have struggled and failed to make your ideas work. Doesn't that discourage you?" He smiled and said, "That's okay. We have to keep trying. We haven't found a cure to cancer yet either. But that doesn't mean we give up."

I viewed the Individual Endeavors as a fresh new take on Sizer's powerful idea. Just as Sizer had envisioned, each of the IP students would identify something interesting to work on, unconstrained by conventional academic topics. This was their moment to pick their own mountain to scale. And at the end, they wouldn't *tell* teachers what they had learned; they'd *show* friends and family, as well as teachers, what they had become good at. But where coalition schools had often, unwittingly, shrunk the projects down to hillocks, IP students would go all in and choose, if not mountains, then steep hills. They'd be ambitious. Instead of tacking their project onto an already fragmented day, picking something doable rather than worthy, or rushing to do it in the last three weeks of their senior year, they'd devote lots of time and energy to it. It would become the centerpiece of their school experience.

However, Dominic's study of the piano stirred up old questions: Were all endeavors of equal educational value? Were there any constraints on what a student might choose to pursue? Some of the other kids had taken on more obvious choices for endeavors: book writing, a review of scientific research, and filmmaking. They involved traditional academic skills, covered large bodies of knowledge, and each rested within a recognizable discipline. But jazz piano?

For me, Dominic's endeavor represented the perfect test case. It was clear that mastering jazz presented a huge challenge to him, and that was essential. Certainly Dominic was taking a risk. What if he didn't get good enough to play in public by the end of the term? His endeavor was difficult—he'd have to sweat to accomplish it. The piano required hours of focused practice. But hard work and challenge weren't enough. Lots of things are difficult and offer the chance of success or failure: tightrope walking, learning the complete chronology of wars in the Western Hemisphere, or memorizing long passages of poetry. Such efforts require hours of study or a great deal of practice, but not necessarily anything else. Yet I had a hunch that jazz was more like book writing or studying science than it was like tightrope walking. What made the difference? When I finally heard Dominic talk about his work and listened to him play, I realized what the difference was. Jazz was complex.

By the time Dominic got his standing ovation, my uncertainty about the criteria for endeavors had been replaced by clarity. His endeavor entailed more than one kind of skill (reading music, composing, *and* performing). The work was meaty.

Finally, as I watched Dominic take the leap and attempt that most difficult aspect of jazz, improvisation in front of an audience, the idea of grit fell into its rightful place. His endeavor elicited not simply diligence, but an *eagerness* to persevere in the face of frustration. Such zeal can emerge only when you are genuinely committed to your goal. Dominic's growing devotion to jazz, his longing to be good at it, and the rich layers of knowledge on which his endeavor rested—these were what elevated his efforts from a nice project to an educational experience that changed him.

My worry with John's proposed Individual Endeavor was the opposite of my worry with Dominic's. He said he wanted to write a philosophical novel. It just seemed way too ambitious for one semester. But again, it wasn't my place to discourage him.

My worry turned out to be unfounded. John finished the first novel early on in the semester, gave it to me to read, and started his second one. By the end of the semester, he was working on a third draft of his second philosophical novel. And his growth as a writer between the two books was phenomenal. It was like seeing someone take steroids for writing.

John doesn't fit the stereotype of the kind of kid schools fail. He's smart, well read, quiet, and thoughtful. Nonetheless, school *was* failing him. He's a reminder that the school system fails all kinds of students. But John, who before the IP never dreamed of education after high school, is now a sophomore in college. And, more important, he's a published author.

The many students who heave, glide, or resist their way through conventional schooling without developing a deep love of some domain and the mastery that usually goes hand-in-hand with such love enter adulthood disabled.

Individual books, periods of history, or math topics may quickly fade from memory. Most adults remember little of what they learned in high school. Psychologists know quite a bit about what it takes to become an expert: layers of knowledge, practice, commitment, trying something and then trying it a different way, and finally, using one's expertise in a range of settings. These are the elements of expertise. They take time. No one becomes an expert overnight or after a few sessions. No one becomes an expert simply by dabbling or by doing a unit in a textbook, filling out worksheets, or hearing what the experts have done from a lecture. When kids know something about a topic (a class in Spanish or history), they may be able to pass a test, but it's not clear anything profound has happened to them. In contrast, when they are experts, they can *do* things: compose music, cater dinners, write books, fix cars, develop arguments, use mathematical thinking to solve real problems, and so on, and that sense of accomplishment and facility is generative. Students who attain hard-won mastery at something they care about want to experience that same process again and again. The research suggests that overall their lives are fuller and more satisfying. And the sense of ownership that comes from such mastery endures.

*   *   *

One day, in the summer after my junior year, I was up at the school doing some batting practice with a friend. It was a day off for me. It had rained all week, so no one needed to water the garden, it wasn't a community volunteer day, and we were still a few days off pickling and freezing vegetables for the school year. It was midsummer, so the school grounds were completely empty, and my friend and I took advantage of this to play some baseball on the school diamond.

After a few hours of taking turns at bat, my friend headed off, and I headed down to the garden to wait for a ride. I was still a few weeks away from being able to drive myself and needed to wait around for my parents to pick me up.

But, as I walked down the hill and crossed the road to the two-acre plot where Project Sprout lived, I was surprised to see that there was a car parked by the farm stand. We never sold our produce, but sometimes we gave some of it away during the summer when we had too much to store or deliver to shelters. I expected that the car's driver was hoping to score some produce, but whoever it was would be disappointed. At the moment, nothing was harvested.

It turned out the driver was a woman in her thirties, and at first I thought she was walking around the garden on her own. It took a moment for me to realize that she was actually holding someone's hand, only that someone had been hidden by the tall tomato plants, because he was four years old. The mom, seeing me, said, "Oh, hi there! I hope we're not intruding."

"Not at all," I said, "but unfortunately we don't have any vegetables to give away today. If you come back on Thurs—"

"Oh no, no, that's okay," she said. "We're not looking for produce. It's just that my son was in one of your after-school programs, and every day we drive by he begs me to stop, and we never seem to have time. But today we do, so I thought I'd let him show me around. As long as we're not in the way, of course," she added.

Sure enough, I recognized her son as Parker Hanes, a four-year-old boy who had come to the garden every day after school for a month in May.

"Absolutely not," I said. "I'm just waiting for a ride. Spend as much time as you want."

So for the next half hour or so, I sat at the edge of the garden while Parker Hanes led his mom by the hand around the garden. Occasionally he would disappear behind a row of tomatoes or a stretch of young corn, but his voice carried through the garden to where I sat.

"Mommy, look, these are my beans. We planted them with the taters so they grow good."

Or, "Mommy, look, look, these are my peas, they have little fingies and they climb and climb and climb until I eat them."

Eventually, Parker's mom got tired of touring. "Come on, honey, time to go. We'll come back another day, though, I promise."

But as they left the garden, he suddenly stopped in his tracks and turned to look up at her. His eyes were wide with a mixture of excitement, fear, and expectancy.

"Mommy," he said. "Do you like my garden?"

I remember looking at little Parker Hanes, his head barely reaching his mom's waist, and then looking out at two acres of farm production. I remember thinking how amazing it was that a four-year-old could feel ownership over something as vast and unwieldy as Project Sprout. And I remember thinking it was even more amazing that he wasn't wrong. He hadn't been tricked into feeling that way. He had been there every day, planting the seeds, watering the sprouts, weeding the rows, and he really was responsible for much of the life there.

It seems almost unnecessary to say that every high school kid should have a chance to feel about something the way Parker Hanes felt about his garden.

We said at the beginning of this chapter that there were ways in which this step was the simplest, the most difficult, and the most important. To require mastery is a very simple step, achievable in a single stroke. Just tell everyone they must become a master of something, and then set up a time when each student will demonstrate his or her mastery. This is, in fact, what Ted Sizer intended with the performances he described, back when he started the Coalition of

Essential Schools. But more often than not, those demonstrations got watered down until they were simply a collection of projects students rushed to finish in time for evaluation. We suggest, instead, putting mastery at the center of your school. Students (and those guiding them) will need to spend time, perhaps several weeks, choosing endeavors that demand expertise. The endeavors must be complex and multilayered. They should involve several kinds of skills, rest on a range of types of knowledge, and be embodied in ways that can be shared with others (books, performances, meals, scientific reports, useful new tools, software, or machines). At the end, students should show (tell, demonstrate, perform) some work that is useful or beautiful to others. Not only that; the students should be able to teach what they now know to novices and trade insights and ideas with other experts.

Mastery that is not given due time and status is a waste, and allowing kids a chance at true mastery requires a big chunk of the school day and school year. But we believe that a school without real mastery fails to prepare kids for their future.

7

OVERCOME OBSTACLES, TOGETHER

The truth is, when it comes to creating a new school, the devil is in the details. There are some problems that you just can't plan for, and some solutions that you shouldn't plan, remedies that students should work out organically as they go along. Mistakes will be made, plans will go awry, group dynamics will shift, and new solutions will be needed. Some of the hardest and most interesting challenges that arose that first year of the IP came as complete surprises.

Elements that seem straightforward may become roadblocks. You may be blindsided by the reaction of a student or teacher. People will behave unpredictably. But any school that can't deviate from the script is not a very good school. In fact, glitches, and students' responses to those glitches, can be some of the most powerful elements of a good education. After all, shouldn't all teens learn, with help, how to deal with the unexpected and how to shift tactics without losing sight of the goal?

In traditional school, obstacles are often viewed as hindrances, embarrassments, things to scurry past as quickly and painlessly as possible. Because your school is run by students, there is the potential for obstacles to be educational opportunities, and the experience of overcoming them can be as rich an education as any other component of the school.

Sarah was the only senior besides me in the Independent Project. I thought, going in, that this would be a reason she could really flourish in the program. She needed fewer credits than the other kids, she had already taken her SATs, and she was in the process of applying to college. In other words, she had fewer burdens, it seemed to me, and therefore would be free to make the most of the IP.

It wasn't just her age. Unlike many of the others, she came into the program already possessing serious interests. She was the star of almost every school play and musical. I once watched her play Sandy in *Grease*, and I thought she was as good as any you might see in a professional production. She was an avid painter and had already taken every art class the school offered, plus a few independent studies. She had a group of close-knit friends among the art crowd. She wasn't very academic, but she was bright and lively. She was applying to high-caliber colleges: Bennington, Oberlin, Sarah Lawrence.

To be honest, among kids like Dominic and Rix, who were on the edge of dropping out of high school, and John, who had diagnosed learning difficulties and had received his fair share of Fs, at the outset, Sarah was the least of my worries.

Early on, I made a couple of big mistakes. Sarah said she wanted to do an independent study with Mrs. Truman, the art teacher.

"The thing is," I told her when she mentioned her idea, "we're not really supposed to be taking classes in the school during the Independent Project."

A look of consternation spread across her face, and she seemed very serious as she said, "But I feel it would be a real shame if I didn't continue to pursue my art because of the Independent Project. Wouldn't it? And I'm at a stage in my art career where the best way to move further is to work with a teacher who really knows her stuff."

"Okay," I thought. "That does make sense." Why should she be discouraged from pursuing her passion in the Independent Project? Wouldn't that be hypocritical? And, yeah, if there was an expert in the school, why not take advantage of that? That was exactly how I hoped teachers would interact with students within the IP.

"Okay, sure," I said. She could carry out an independent study in art during the semester.

Then, sometime during the first week, Sarah said that she was auditioning for the role of Macbeth in the school's annual Shakespeare production.

"Sam," she said on Friday of de-orientation, "I'm thinking I'll do an Individual Endeavor related to my role as Macbeth. I want to really get *into* the character."

It sounded like a bad idea to me. In my mind, Macbeth was something she was already doing, in addition to school, and so should be separate from her work in the IP. I figured that it would be a cop-out if she just counted her commitment to the play as her Individual Endeavor.

"I don't think that's a good idea, Sarah. This is an opportunity to do something new—something different from what you're already doing." I understand my thinking at the time. But it was probably wrong.

Still, despite these mistakes, in the beginning things looked good. The first week of academics Sarah taught us how Pixar animation works. Her presentation was energetic and engaging, filled with detail that was clearly the product of serious research. She taught us with joy and vigor, and I think everyone agreed it was the best forty minutes of teaching that first week. I remember thinking that Sarah would be a tent pole that would help raise the standard of the group throughout the semester.

But Sarah never regained the level of passion, commitment, hard work, or interest that she had that first week. In fact, she was our one failure. I still don't completely understand why, and I suppose I never will. But I know a lot of the factors that contributed to it, including plenty of my own mistakes.

For one, I think letting her do the independent study was a mistake. Allowing her to pursue art was not a mistake, but I should have either encouraged her to choose an art-related Individual Endeavor or allowed her to carve out time to do art during the day and on a case-by-case basis work with a supervisor. The problem was that the independent study just ended up being a continuation of her art classes so far in high school. And I found out from her teacher, too late in the game, that that consisted largely of hanging out with her friends in the art room. It took her away from both her Individual Endeavor and the academics, without pushing her in new directions or challenging her in any way.

More and more, as the semester went on, she disappeared to the art room to work on her independent study. It was only when the art teacher started coming to me and asking where Sarah was that I realized she wasn't going to the art room at all—she was just leaving school with her friends. It turned out she was using the independent study to say she had to leave the IP, and the IP to say she had to leave the art room.

On a deeper level, the independent study disconnected her from the group and the program. The rest of us didn't have some outside commitment that could pull us away. So if someone was fucking around, we knew, and we called them out on it. This was harder to do with Sarah, because she was more disconnected and had commitments elsewhere.

Second, it became apparent (again, way too late in the game) that preventing her from making her Individual Endeavor about Macbeth was a mistake. She was really passionate about the role and ended up using her time in the afternoon to memorize lines and learn more about the play, rather than work on her Individual Endeavor. But because it *wasn't* her Individual Endeavor, she couldn't really devote all her time to it like she wanted to, and she missed out on an opportunity to expand beyond the boundaries set by just playing the role.

Instead, her Individual Endeavor was to write a play. But I never saw her working on it. Or at least, I could never tell the difference between her working on it and her working on memorizing her lines. And she always had a reason why she couldn't show it to anyone. It wasn't ready. She wanted to type it up first. She was about to make a big change to the plot. Then again, Dominic was never willing to play the piano for us until the end, so why was that necessarily a bad thing?

I guess because there were other warning signs. One Friday she couldn't really teach us about her science question because she wasn't quite done with it.

"Guys, you're really gonna love this stuff—it's just sooo interesting. But it's just too good to teach it to you before I know a little bit more. I'll do it next week, okay?"

But the next Friday she was sick and didn't come in. One week, she couldn't take part in the book discussion because her cat had died and she was really torn up.

"I want to guys, I really do," she said, sniffling. "I just need to be on my own today, okay?"

All of these on their own were valid excuses. But I should have pieced them together to make a bigger picture.

It's not as though I ignored it completely. Actually, Mr. Huron and I talked about it all the time. During the semester, we would meet every day before school and after school, just to chat about how things were going. Most days we also ended up meeting again, during the day, to address something specific, and there were some days when we met throughout the day. Sarah was fully on our radar as someone to worry about. Still, we felt we couldn't help but accept her excuses. I mean, what were we gonna say? "Get over your stupid dead cat"?

I can't speak for Mr. Huron, but I think the real reason I didn't address Sarah head-on sooner is that deep down I was afraid. The more she fucked up, the more I worried that she was proof that the Independent Project didn't work. I was scared to address the issue because everyone else was doing so well. I thought that if I pretended nothing was wrong with Sarah, then I could feel good about everything.

And in the end, it wasn't me who decided something needed to be done. Around two-thirds of the way through the semester, the group spoke up. At that point, Sarah often missed Friday teachings, missed school altogether, spent the day in the art room, sat silently in the corner. She chose our second book, *The Importance of Being Earnest*, but then didn't read anyone else's. So one day, when Sarah had once again missed morning check-in, Tim spoke up. We were all sitting around the table when he said, "Listen, Sam. We've been talking. We want to have an intervention with Sarah. It's really not fair to the rest of us that she doesn't do any work. She's bringing the whole program down. We don't want the IP to fail because of her."

I was surprised. I had been so focused on Sarah, I hadn't thought about how the rest of the group might feel about it.

"Does everyone feel this way?" I said.

They nodded. Clearly they had talked about it already. "It's not just what Tim said, though that's part of it," said John. "It's also not right for us to let her just throw the semester away."

I had no idea the group was so upset by her lack of commitment. But they were. They took it as a personal offense when she didn't do her work. So Mr. Huron and I talked about it, and we decided that we would have an intervention, as long as we could all agree on certain ground rules. No character assassinations. Focus not on the *way* she was, but on what she had *done*. And focus not on her, but on how it made each of us feel. The group agreed. And actually, I was amazed by how tactful, honest, and direct they were when talking to Sarah.

She cried. She told us how much we all meant to her, that all she had ever wanted to do was impress us, that she felt like she always let us down and that nothing she did was ever good enough for us. Several people in the group were touched and felt really bad about the whole thing.

But Mr. Huron and I experienced it differently. We saw a side of Sarah neither of us had seen before, or at least had ever been willing to admit was there. She was deceitful and manipulative, and it worried both of us. It was a turning point but, as I said, one that came too late. We started to realize how much of what she had told us wasn't true. Many of her lies started to unravel. Her art teacher said she had barely done any work. We decided it was time to confront her about her Individual Endeavor, and she admitted to having done nothing.

When it finally came time to do our public presentations of our Individual Endeavors, she sat onstage and talked about her life and about how even though she hadn't succeeded in doing an Individual Endeavor, by failing she had learned a lot about herself, more than she had in the rest of her life. Many members of the audience were clearly moved, impressed by her honesty, courage, and boldness. But the other Indies and I were embarrassed and frustrated.

Mr. Huron and I talked at length about how to handle it.

"We need to fail her," I said.

"No," said Mr. Huron. "That wouldn't be right. If we fail her, Oberlin might revoke her acceptance. We don't want to ruin her life."

"But if we pass her, it will be a kick in the face to the other Indies. It will undermine the whole program," I said.

"We can fail her," he said, "with the option of gaining a partial passing credit if she presents us with a completed Individual Endeavor."

It didn't totally make sense to me, because the IP wasn't just about completing an endeavor. She couldn't make up for months of not doing work, of not doing the academics, of lying to us. At the same time, I didn't want her to not go to college because of the IP. That would be backward. In the end, she gave us a binder full of partially completed scenes of a play, and we gave her partial credit.

Like I said, I still don't know what went wrong, not entirely. The fact that she was a senior, had all her credits, and was accepted early decision into college halfway through the semester all turned out to be bad things, not good things. But that's not to say seniors could never do the IP, because someone else could have made the most of that (after all, I was a senior). It was a mistake to let her do the independent study, I think. But I have no way of knowing for sure. And it might have been better if her Individual Endeavor had been related to the thing she was already committing so much time to, but again, who knows how it would have played out.

Mr. Huron has always stood by the fact that he's glad she did the IP her senior year. She had coasted through high school, making up excuses, skirting around failure using manipulation and deceit. And the IP was the first time she had to really face it, had to let failure sit on her lap. He thinks that it will have a good impact on her life, much more so than another semester of coasting through independent studies. I'm still not sure.

One thing I do know for sure is that I don't believe her story means
that the Independent Project doesn't work. I don't even think it reveals
a certain "type" for which it will fail. Another kid fitting her profile
could have succeeded. I think it points out that no school will ever
work for everyone, every year. That's just impossible. And rather than
being afraid of addressing failure, like I was, we should have tackled
and grappled with problems like this head-on, from the beginning,
because if we had done that, we could have helped a lot more.

Sarah first trickled into my awareness somewhere in early September.
Sam's first stories about her sketched a jubilant and articulate young
woman, brimming with the kind of enthusiasm that seemed a perfect
fit for the Independent Project. But the Sarah anecdotes soon shifted.
She came late, he said. She hadn't answered her science question that
week. She changed her mind about her Individual Endeavor. She cried.
Hearing these bits and pieces, I wanted to come to school, find the girls'
locker room, give Sarah a good pinch, and leave. I've been teaching adolescents for a long time. I know a young diva when I see one.

As her behavior got more outrageous, Sam seemed more beside
himself. And hearing the fragments that came my way, I wished Sam
would come down hard on her, and sooner rather than later. I fumed
that Mr. Huron wasn't stepping in. I couldn't understand why the group
was so forbearing. But I was on the outside, a mere spectator. Sam
waved off my unsolicited comments, explaining that it was a process. I
had to pipe down. But I ground my teeth, tapped my foot, and imagined
myself striding in there and setting her straight.

I have never been consistent in my views about teenagers. I love
their vibrant energy, their outsized claims and hubris, and their endear-
ing uncertainty. But I hate how self-absorbed they can be, how shallow
they can seem, and how taken they are with their own sorrows and
grievances. I have very little tolerance for brattiness. I hated watching
this petulant girl not do what she was supposed to.

Somewhere in those early days, when Sarah's storminess bubbled
up and became a serious problem for the IP, I remembered something

from forty years before, when I was a girl. My own brother had been a turbulent teenager. Smart, energetic, talented, and engaging, he was also manipulative, resented rules, and had an overpowering hunger for nearly every possible sensation. He got into all kinds of conflicts and jams. That was the sixties, and in a family like mine, it was never clear whether rebellion was a sign of strong-mindedness and political courage or just a sign of trouble. At some point, when my brother was flunking a course at his elite boarding school, my father said, in a lofty and confident tone that impressed my mother (even though they were divorced), "Failure is not an option." Everyone in the family nodded. Good response. Failure is not an option. Only, a few months later my brother got kicked out of that school, mid-term. My father was wrong. Failure is always an option. And for many teenagers, school failure seems less awful than whatever is plaguing them.

One approach for dealing with students who fail in one way or another, championed by some psychologists, policy makers, and school principals, is to hold all kids to exacting codes of conduct. A student hits another kid? He's suspended. A student doesn't do the work in a class? She flunks and retakes the class. A student is rude to her teacher? She goes to detention. A student has trouble learning the material? He flunks and retakes the class. A student skips class on a regular basis? She goes to detention. A student has trouble making friends and gets into fights? He gets suspended. A student has a drug problem? She gets suspended. See the crazy pattern here? Very different kinds of problems are all funneled through a narrow set of solutions. The real catch, however, is that they're not actually solutions. They're just consequences.

When I stood back and began to think about that somewhat limited set of options, used all across the country, I realized what they all had in common was that they entailed excluding kids from the very institution we had created to guide them through a vulnerable and pivotal moment in development. Even the solutions that don't appear to involve banishment, like giving an F, often end up having the impact of pushing kids toward the periphery of the community. One of two things is likely to happen there at the periphery. Either kids begin to dis-identify with high school or they form a new community with all the other kids at the periphery. Neither is an ideal outcome.

And yet, what are schools to do when kids screw up? The problem facing Sam, the other IP students, and Mr. Huron was no different. Should Sarah fail or be supported? Should they work harder to draw her in, or should they kick her out?

Dennis Littky fervently believes that the more trouble a kid is having, the more included she must be. In the public high schools he founded in Providence, Rhode Island, kids who screw up are given even more one-on-one time with a devoted teacher, lots of encouragement (and pushing) to follow through on projects, and lots of support (and pressure) from their peers. Littky's teachers call kids at night to see what they're up to, drive them to the grocery store, get to know their families— each and every one of those teachers is instructor *and* social worker.

Littky isn't the only one to have used this approach. In almost every town there are devoted teachers and guidance counselors who live by that same principle: that the more trouble a kid is having, the more time and attention that kid needs. Often that attention is part friendship ("Let's shoot some hoops after school"; "I brought in this CD I thought you'd like"; "Why not stop in here and eat lunch with me?"), part practical support ("I've arranged for you to take the late bus so you can work on the school newspaper"; "I called your parents—they agreed to let you try out for volleyball"), and part stern taskmaster ("You've been wasting my time and yours—get with the program"; "I'm disappointed in your work recently; what's going on?"). When a kid really likes a teacher and wants to be liked in return, she is much more likely to respond well to admonishments, consequences, and expressions of disappointment.

But there are two drawbacks to Littky's approach. One is that teachers who throw themselves so fully into the lives of their students burn out or cannot possibly help every kid who needs it. The great advantage of the Independent Project was that for every kid in trouble, there were seven other kids who could push, cajole, support, and chastise her.

But the other problem with the Littky approach is that not every kid who screws up in school comes from a difficult family life or is hampered by poverty, immigration problems, addiction, or undiagnosed learning disabilities. Some kids, like Sarah, behave badly for other reasons. They don't know how to persevere. They don't yet feel they need to. They are self-indulgent and no one has ever insisted they buckle down and do what's required rather than what they're in the mood for.

A pause here, to talk about what might seem like a contradiction. A core idea behind the IP is that students will get a better education if they have a strong voice in what and how they learn, and have the chance to study things that are interesting to them, things that they feel matter. So you might be surprised to hear both of us suggest that Sarah shouldn't have been allowed to do whatever she wanted. The disparity between what we are advocating and what Sarah did that fall may seem slight, but it's not. It's an ocean of difference.

Sarah tended to believe that whatever impulses or thoughts seemed pressing to her on a given day should guide her actions. In contrast, the IP was asking students to make deliberate and considered decisions about what to work on and what goals to set themselves. Once they had made those decisions, there was enormous collective pressure on them to see their goals through to the end. IP sought self-governance; Sarah seemed drawn to self-indulgence.

Sarah was bright, talented, and appealing. She grew up in a loving middle-class family (her father was an educator). She just didn't think she needed to toe the line. She loved taking center stage. She wanted drama. For her, puberty had just amplified her personality, exponentially.

Watching the drama of Sarah unfold, I began to think that there were two kinds of failure among high school students, and they required two kinds of responses. Kids like Sarah should be brought up short. The Independent Project was supposed to be appealing—an educational opportunity to be relished. If a student didn't value what it offered—choice, autonomy, responsibility, learning from peers, intellectual depth—she should return to the more standard options.

The other kind of failure was not really failure—it was struggle. A student like Dominic wanted to succeed but stumbled over some of the steps. He had difficulty focusing, was inexperienced at following through, and feared tackling complex material. Those were problems the group should embrace and work with.

The award-winning journalist and historian David Halberstam often told the story of getting fired from his first job writing for a newspaper, and the winding path it took him to get his second job writing for a newspaper. The way he told it, getting fired was a setback, not a failure. He never wavered in his desire to become a newspaper writer—he just had trouble navigating the steps that would get him there.

Sarah didn't face a setback; she screwed up. And she should have been forced, much earlier in the term, to choose whether to stay and work or leave. Kids like Dominic and Rix, who periodically struggled with specific features of the program, faced setbacks and needed help and encouragement to forge ahead, like David Halberstam.

My hunch is that programs that seem so rewarding to most kids, even when they falter (like Mirabelle, Dominic, or Sam), don't need to focus too much on punishment. Most kids will do what Halberstam did. They'll persevere. And when they falter, they'll have peers to shore them up. Leaving would be the worst punishment, and they'll do what they have to in order to stay in the project. The kids who would just as soon leave, like Sarah, should leave.

I talked earlier about Mirabelle's struggles when we switched from the sciences to the languages. What I didn't say was that, compared to pretty much everyone else, Mirabelle's switch was smooth sailing. In the first two weeks of the languages I thought I might be watching the death of the Independent Project.

By the end of the sciences, the group (with the exception of Sarah, of course) was energized, passionate, engaged, and working really, really hard. Everyone agreed that they had finally discovered what it was like to love school and love learning. I was happy, excited, and enjoying school more than I ever had before. And then we started the languages.

The literary portion was great. We read seven novels and a play. I had taken honors and AP English all through high school, and in that one half semester I read more novels for school than I had in the rest of high school put together. Two of our members read more novels that semester than in their whole lives. No, it wasn't the English language that was a problem. It was the mathematical one.

It turned out that the one thing the whole group had in common was a pure hatred of math. We started with *Flatland*. That part was okay. People liked the story. We had some good discussions about it. But I had hoped that *Flatland* would provide a segue into the rest of mathematics, that it would serve as a vehicle for demonstrating that math could be interesting and fun and not just about calculations and procedures.

That didn't happen. The problem was that a very specific approach to mathematics (memorizing formulas and mindlessly carrying out calculations) had become so ingrained at that point that the rest of the group didn't see any connection between *Flatland* and math.

And despite my arguments otherwise, they couldn't be convinced. So on the following Monday, when I said, okay, everyone should pick a topic in math to explore this week, they all groaned.

"This is bullshit," said Dominic. "This is just like regular school all over again." Everyone seemed to agree. By forcing them to do math, they said, I was making the same mistake that I had criticized so heavily in traditional school. I tried to argue that it was different. I had criticized the long list of required specific and arbitrary content. But everyone believes *some* things should be required in school. We might disagree on what those things are, but we all have something in mind that every kid should learn.

"Okay, yeah, fair enough," they said. We all agreed that kids should learn to read in school. Most people thought that everyone should learn about specific atrocities of the past, like the Holocaust. I tried to make the logical next step to math.

"So, I designed the Independent Project, and *I believe* that everyone should learn how to think like a mathematician. I'm not prescribing specific mathematical knowledge, just the ability to use logic, and appreciate how problems can be solved using math, and maybe get a glimpse at what it's like to describe nature with the language of mathematics."

The group didn't agree. "That's just 'cause you like math," said Tim. "The rest of us don't see why it's important for us to learn it."

Mirabelle tried to be helpful at this point. "You mean because of, like, shopping for groceries and paying bills and stuff? Like, I guess it's important for all of us to be able to use math in our lives."

But that wasn't the point. "I don't care so much about you using math because it has a practical purpose. Being comfortable with numbers is probably really helpful in life, but I doubt you'll learn that in half a semester. But I think, at the very least, being able to appreciate how math is used, understand how those who use it do it, and having a go at the kinds of thinking involved in math, is all really important."

But my arguments fell on deaf ears. Almost no math was done that week. And everyone's frustration and resentment trickled over into the rest of the school day. The group became surly and grumpy. Morale fell, and I noticed people working less on their Individual Endeavors. I felt the Independent Project slipping between my fingers. The teachers from the CSC were right all along. We were able to work hard for a while, but eventually kids would give up without an adult pushing them along.

Dominic was particularly moody. I think he felt betrayed. Like, somehow, I had tricked him into doing this program, and for the first few months led him to believe he could actually enjoy school and be a good student, and then dropped this bomb on him. Like science was a honey trap for math.

On Thursday morning, during check-in, when I brought up the fact that tomorrow was Friday and we were supposed to be teaching each other math stuff, Dominic lashed out. "I don't want to. It's bullshit. None of us want to do this." I looked around, hoping someone would come to my defense, hoping that maybe Tim or Mirabelle would ask Dominic to buck up. But no one said anything; they just looked down in silent affirmation. And I finally lost my temper.

"You know what? Fuck *you* guys." Everyone looked shocked. Hell, I had shocked myself. But I was still angry. "You were happy to sing the Independent Project's praises when it was going well for you, when you were succeeding, but as soon as we hit a little speed bump, you jump ship and bail on me. As soon as the going gets tough, you guys decide I fucked up and it's not worth your time. I would have thought you guys would at least try. I thought the least you could do was give it a go."

I was a little embarrassed by my outburst. I left the locker room and went to see a math teacher in my school. She had taught me math since I was thirteen; she was a brilliant teacher, one of the early support-ers of the Independent Project, and, most important, a good friend. I went to her hoping she could give me advice on how to overcome our math hurdle. Her best advice was to just keep trying, and try to help the other Indies find ways in which math could be interesting to them.

The next day, at check-in, I said that we weren't going to do any teaching that day. Instead, we were just going to help each other find math topics that might be interesting to us. I apologized for getting angry at them the day before. And to my surprise, they apologized back.

"I hate math," said Tim. "But the Independent Project has changed my life. I think I can give it a go, if it's important to the IP."

By Monday, everyone had found something they were going to try. I had suggested to Dominic that he look into the math of poker be-cause I knew he loved cards. It turned out he was fascinated by it. One by one, everyone found something they could explore. And week by week, bit by bit, people started working harder on their math.

I wish I could pinpoint some clever trick I landed on that jump-started the group's investment in their math work. But, truthfully, I don't think there was one single thing, one turning point, and it defi-nitely wasn't something I did. Yeah, I think my outburst had an impact on them, albeit unintentionally. But that, on its own, would only have gotten them to work for a few days. They might have felt guilty and wanted to do it for me, but if that was their only reason for moving forward, it would have faded quickly. Instead, the Indies kept working on math for the rest of the semester, choosing new topics each week. Tim explored the math of music; Dakota became fixated on trigonometry; Erik returned to infinity and eventually cardinality (though he didn't realize it, he gave himself a crash course in some basic set theory).

I think the biggest reason things changed was that the responsibility was on their shoulders. In the beginning, the fact that there were no teachers, no one in charge, meant they could spend a week and a half doing nothing, with nobody around to enforce anything. But with time, that also meant no one was going to swoop in and come up with a clever way for them to get motivated. And no one could finally say, "Okay, fine, don't worry about it, I'll cut you some slack." It was all on their shoulders, and they were either going to get on with it or not. I think as that slowly dawned on them, they realized they had nothing to push back against, no one to disobey, and so they just started working.

One of my many weaknesses as a mom has been my compulsive need to solve problems and make things right for my kids. I always told myself, when they were little, that it was good to jump in and help them make things better, that they would learn from me that you don't need to succumb, or settle, that when something is going badly, you can act! Maybe that helped sometimes. But it also meant that my sons didn't often get to figure things out for themselves. Equally important, I robbed them of the chance to learn how to simply endure rough spots. So when Sam hit that math wall, I desperately wanted to help him figure out how to make math come alive. He seemed panicked, as if screwing up the math portion would sink the whole ship. I hated watching him panic, and I arrogantly, naïvely, always think there's a solution to every classroom problem. But this time I knew there wasn't one thing I could do to help. And for once, I realized that for him, the struggle over math was the best educational experience he could have. He thrashed around, trying to figure out whether to give up on math, bring in some cool new book, go back to basics, yell at them, or offer them more fun and encouragement. His relentless worry was a thing to behold.

And here's what I learned watching Sam thrash around: we educators spend far too much time trying to clear away the problems that kids face. When they think something is boring, we either raise the stakes for not learning it ("This is boring or hard, but if you don't do it, you'll fail, stay after school, get a low grade, not get into college") or we try to dress it up ("This is boring or hard, so we'll add some pretty pictures, let you make a collage, hand out candy after the test, let you spend five minutes watching YouTube if you do your homework"). What we rarely do is sit with the problem and let them sit with it. Usually if a kid or group of kids is struggling with something, the struggle is meaningful. The kids in the IP stalled, backtracked, wasted time, and argued with one another, Sam as much or more than the others. He dove into the math problem, and ultimately they dove in with him. Whatever math they didn't cover because he couldn't quickly or easily solve the problem of their resistance was replaced by something that had a much more lasting impact—the experience of figuring out how to get unstuck.

The first two examples of obstacles we had to overcome were not that unusual. After all, you might expect that in any school some students will struggle more than others, and the group will reach low points. But I want to give you one other example, one that highlights how quirky and unpredictable some obstacles turn out to be.

You know now where the Independent Project's home was: the coach's office of the girls' locker room. It had been hard enough acquiring any space at all; I never expected that we might run into problems with the space we *did* acquire.

Fall was volleyball season, and every day when the final bell rang, we packed up our stuff as quickly as possible and darted out of the locker room. Once we were out, Coach Biggins would give the okay to the team, they would file in, and he'd head into his office. Apart from a few giggles from the girls' volleyball team the first few times we vacated the locker room, it was all as smooth as could be.

Then winter came and, with it, basketball season. Our school had a long history of successful girls' basketball, and the coach was a real old-timer, who'd been coaching the team for nearly twenty years. I had known him forever—I played baseball with one of his relatives, co-captained the varsity basketball team with another, and played on a team coached by his nephew. So every day when I'd slip out of the locker room past him, I'd smile and say "hi." He never returned the smile or the "hi," and I figured he was just old and grumpy and focused on winning.

But, slowly, it trickled down to me through the school rumor mill that he hated the fact that we had been allowed to use the coach's office. He thought it was an atrocity, a disgrace to the name of high school basketball everywhere. Soon I didn't need the rumors to know he didn't like us. I'd come in in the morning to find our books tossed into the corner of the room or someone's papers shoved into the trash.

Finally, I brought it up with Mr. Huron, who knew the family well and was a longtime high school coach himself.

"I didn't want to mention it to you," he said, "because it shouldn't be on your radar. But since you know, yes, he's a little upset. He's said that you leave a mess and move his stuff around, and he thinks you play with the basketballs."

It was true that every morning we moved the rack of basketballs into the corner of the room so that we had space to work and talk. From then on, at the end of the day, the group did a thorough cleaning of the room and moved the basketballs right back to where we found them. I assumed that, despite his continued grumpy greetings, the problem had been solved.

That was, until Mr. Huron took me into his office one morning. "Coach Pacetti is making a request to have you moved. I'm not sure if it will go through, but he has some sway in the school, and I wanted you to know."

"I want to meet him, then," I said.

Mr. Huron didn't think that was a good idea.

"Come on," I said. "If he wants us to leave, then he can at least tell me to my face."

Mr. Huron reluctantly agreed to arrange a meeting.

Coach Pacetti was angry. He could barely look at me when we talked. He muttered something about us making a mess, and I promised him we would work even harder to keep ourselves to ourselves. He muttered something about the basketballs, and I promised him we didn't touch them. Finally, he muttered something about his twenty years as a coach, bringing this school to the western Mass championship however many times.

"Coach," I said. "You know I respect you and the program you've built. But this is eight kids' high school education. We're not going to leave." We stayed.

This story highlights that you can never predict all the problems that will come up. People will doubt your school, those you expect to support it won't, basketball coaches will wage war against you, parts of your curriculum will falter, and students will fail.

But this kind of school lends itself to adapting to changes, dealing with problems, and inventing new ways for students to learn. The kids take the lead, and it becomes their responsibility to fix issues and overcome challenges. And in doing so, they learn key lessons and skills that are absent from traditional school.

Problems, in your new school, become a part of the curriculum.

to *The Importance of Being Earnest*. We were reading the first draft of John's new novel and watching a rough cut of Tim's film (which made Mirabelle cry), and I was fussing over the final zombie fight in my novella, *Exit Sign*.

For a period of time, however brief, we fell in love with school, with learning, with ideas, with working hard, with teaching one another.

There was just one more element we needed—to reconnect students to their community.

We had set aside the last three weeks of the Independent Project for the Collective Endeavor. The only requirement for the endeavor was that it had to be truly collaborative, and it had to have a positive impact on the community. That community could be the town, the county, the country, or the world, anything broader than the school itself.

Perhaps unsurprisingly, the driving force behind including a Collective Endeavor in the Independent Project was Project Sprout. It was there that I learned what happens when a high school really connects to the community around it.

Project Sprout couldn't stand on the hard work of high school students alone. We needed shovels, seeds, compost, mulch, rakes, and wheelbarrows. We needed volunteers, fencing, sheds, and expertise. We needed money, guidance, and building commission approvals. We needed people to come to our events, bring their kids to our garden, eat our tomatoes. We needed somewhere to start our seedlings in the winter, metal stakes, a water catchment system, and a restaurant to host our pig roast. And all that had to come from the community.

In four years, I saw the community rally around the garden, and saw the school, the kids, and the people around us all benefit from it. By senior year, it was hard to get into a good flow digging beds, because so many of the cars that drove by the garden would honk.

So it was in the garden that I learned how valuable it was for a school to connect with its community. Project Sprout would have been literally impossible to maintain single-handedly. There were two acres of cultivation to look after (in addition to school and sports and a job);

8

OPEN YOUR DOOR TO THE COMMUNITY

It's ironic that just as young people step across the threshold into the adult community, we separate them from it almost entirely. High school should be the bridge to the adult world, not the waiting room for it.

Your doors should be open all year long. Bringing in experts from outside the school, engaging in apprenticeships, teaching kids in the lower schools, teaching adults in the community, collaborating with local businesses—these should all be a regular part of your school from day one.

But you need something more as well—something that requires the whole group, and that has a significant impact on the community. In the Independent Project, this took the form of the Collective Endeavor, the last thing the students did that school year. We think it's a good way to finish—a good last step. Doesn't it make sense that the product of your education all year long would be the ability to come together with your peers and your community to achieve something great?

All that semester, I was immersed in the day in and day out of the Independent Project. I was listening to Dakota teach us about the properties of cellulose, watching Mirabelle present about the origins of art, and following Dominic as he showed us the edible plants around the school. We had an animated discussion about the end of Vonnegut's *Sirens of Titan*, tried to understand Dominic's odds with each hand in a game of poker, and listened to Tim act out his one-man play response there was an annual budget of $20,000 that had to be raised; there was coordination with the cafeterias, scheduling deliveries, organizing events, arranging classes, teaching after-school programs, building sheds and greenhouses. Like many worthy endeavors in life, it could be achieved only by really successful collaboration.

And finally, it was through Project Sprout that I saw how valuable it was for a group of high schoolers to work tirelessly to make their community a better place. The people who served on the board of Project Sprout went on to Yale, Stanford, Middlebury, Cornell. Every single one of them is now working, either in college or as graduates, to do something good in the world. I think that is one of Project Sprout's most important impacts—the effect it had on those of us who were caretakers of that garden for a few brief years. In short, I learned more than anyone could ever expect to learn in high school about working with other people to achieve a goal. And, it seemed, a Collective Endeavor could offer some of that to the Indies.

I had no idea what the Independent Project students would choose as a Collective Endeavor. I floated Project Sprout as an example. We had only three weeks in the IP, so we wouldn't be able to do anything that expansive in scope. But we could do something similar, on a smaller scale, to a similar effect. We could come up with a plan to clean up the local river, and even start executing that plan. We could improve food distribution among local shelters. We could draw up designs to make the school carbon-neutral. We could build a new jungle gym for the park in town. Anything, really. The options were endless.

During Sam's years with Project Sprout, he learned "more than anyone could ever expect to" about how to work with others. I would put it differently. I think he learned more than most teenagers in our culture are ever *allowed* to learn about working in a group.

We're so sure they can't that we never ask them to. And part of that is because it's not the side most adolescents show us. They seem to swim in a bath of self: "How do I feel?" "What do I seem like to others?" "Why are they doing this to *me*?" "Why do I have bad luck?" "I'm

so awesome, everyone is noticing me," "Not enough people are noticing me." You can see this on any street of any small town in America,
where teens seem completely oblivious to everyone but themselves
and the other teens they are hanging out with. When they are de-
lighted with themselves, they laugh and dance down the street as if no
one has ever been so cool, so funny, so impressive, and so powerful.
When they are low, they spread their gloom around them as if shoot-
ing it out of a fog machine, as if the whole world stinks because they
feel bad. Their apparent self-absorption can be incredibly frustrating
for parents, irritating to older brothers and sisters, and unacceptable to
employers. Years ago, psychologists began to describe it as the second
toddlerhood—a time of intense egocentrism.

And though teenagers do love one another with a kind of fervor
not seen during other phases of life, that doesn't mean it's good for
them to be separated from everyone else. Yet you wouldn't know that
from looking around at where we put our high schools. By and large,
we build separate buildings for our teenagers, placing them as far as
possible from the center of the villages and even from the elementary and middle schools. Though schools in cities are often close to
other buildings, the barrier between what happens in the school and
what happens in the rest of the community might as well be two miles
long. I know there are some sensible reasons for this: they need playing
fields and parking, and it's best not to tempt them to skip class. But it
also means that they are spending most of their days exclusively with
kids their own age. The only adults they see are focused almost totally
on guiding them, instructing them, and disciplining them. They are not
around younger children whom they might help care for; they are not
around preteens whom they might mentor. They are not around adults
who might just be friends. We've created a teen ghetto, which isn't
good for anyone.

In the garden, Sam and his friends worked with little kids, with
grown-ups, and with one another. All of them had something to contribute. Having to figure out who was doing what each day, how to

play to one another's strengths, when to back off and let another take charge—lessons in collaboration like these cannot be learned on an occasional Friday afternoon. You can't simply tell kids that collaboration is valuable. Like any complex and important set of skills, the strands that go into cooperating must be learned through practice, and kids need lots of that practice. They need to collaborate day in and day out.

But the kids who built the garden didn't depend solely on one another. That wouldn't have been enough. Few of them knew how to garden on that scale. None of them had turned up a field before, and they didn't have the equipment they needed to do it. They knew nothing about planting complementary vegetables that helped fight bugs and disease. They had no idea how to grow for meals served in a cafeteria to twelve hundred kids. For this they needed something other than one another's help and good energy. They needed other people, people beyond the school walls: cooks, farmers, ecologists, and, yes, bankers and businesspeople to help them get going. The garden built a bridge between the school and the community. And people in the community suddenly saw an authentic way to help the students in the local high school. They didn't need to be volunteer teachers, and they didn't for the most part need to reach into their wallets. They just had to offer their expertise and their willingness to be partners in a project that everyone cared about.

Those intense social connections are exactly what Sam wanted to re-create by requiring a Collective Endeavor. But as he has said, the collective effort needs to be for something that has meaning beyond a good grade.

Luckily, the social impulse that runs at such a fever pitch in adolescence is not only an impulse to be with one another. Teenagers also have a rumbling hunger to have an impact on the broader world. My student Manuel (the future immigration lawyer whose parents had emigrated from Mexico) told me that day over coffee that to get from a trailer park in Texas to Williams College, grit wouldn't have gotten him far if he hadn't also had "something in mind." But he didn't stop there. "Yeah, in high school I knew I would do whatever it took to get to law school. But that's not really what propelled me forward, out of the trailer park onto the Williams campus. It's not enough to have just anything in mind. Not all goals are equal. You need to have something in mind for others."

Manuel had "something in mind for others" because he was raised in a family that emphasized good deeds. But what about all the teens who don't seem to have something in mind for others? Where do they get such a sense of social purpose? It can, and should, be in high school. It begins by allowing them to be useful.

Ironically, our society has increasingly prevented kids from feeling useful by protecting them from work. This impulse is well intentioned and reasonable. In order to develop their fullest capacities, kids need time to develop, both intellectually and emotionally. By and large, researchers have found that longer adolescence is linked to a higher level of personal development. The stereotype of the admirable kid who not only goes to school but has a job delivering papers or working at the corner grocery store to help his family glosses over the truth—kids who work too much are less likely to thrive academically. The day has only so many hours in it, and even an energetic sixteen-year-old has limits to his energy. The more he works at the grocery store, or taking care of his little brother, the less time he has to read, study for class, practice the oboe, play in the chess club, or do martial arts. School is better for teens than working in a factory or taking care of siblings.

However, that doesn't mean it's good for high schoolers to feel that their work has no value to others. There's no inherent reason why becoming more knowledgeable, more cultivated, better at thinking requires teenagers to do work that has no meaning outside of providing them with a good grade. Students shouldn't have to choose between being useful and opening their intellectual horizons. They can, instead, acquire skills and knowledge in the course of making their communities better. They need to feel that what they are learning not only will lead to good things for themselves, but also will lead to good things for others.

Because it wasn't only the sense of collaboration that thrilled the kids in Project Sprout. It was the daily gratification they got from doing something that made a difference—providing food for the cafeteria, the sense that they were reducing their carbon footprint, and the profound joy of bringing good produce to those on food stamps. The garden grew because it fed on one of the most powerful impulses of the teen years—the impulse to make a mark. Why shouldn't school build on that impulse?

Sam included the Collective Endeavor in his design because of the life-changing experience he had with Project Sprout. He had been blown away by how different his friends and classmates seemed when they were working on something that had significance beyond their school walls. He saw that the kid who dragged herself into English class, or skipped homeroom to have a smoke, or borrowed someone else's homework to leave time for a party, instead showed up before school to harvest, after school to work with the first graders, and in a rainstorm to make sure the new greenhouse was set up. Their commitment, sense of responsibility, willingness to sacrifice time and effort to help out were all exponentially higher when they were making something for the larger world, the world beyond their own circle of friends.

The garden he and the other kids created lies along the route I take from our home in southern Berkshire County to Williams College, where I teach. In March and April of that first year, I'd pass by and see him alone out there in the dirt, often in terrible weather, rototilling, putting up fences, trying to build an irrigation system. By late May, however, I'd drive by and see a few of the kids from his baseball team planting seeds, a handful of kids from the remedial classes out there hoeing, or the kids from AP biology tying up tomato plants. On Saturdays I'd see volunteers from the community. Not just farmers, but artists, carpenters, arborists, mechanics, doctors, and nurses.

By mid-July, when school had been in recess for several weeks, the school building had the slightly stale and empty look of summer vacation. No buses in the parking lot, no kids bouncing or slinking their way into or out of the building, no teachers lingering to talk by the cars. But when I turned the corner onto the street where the garden lay, there were seven teenagers, kids who didn't ordinarily hang out together, harvesting, eating cherry tomatoes, and packing up lettuce for the local food kitchen. It was sometimes hard for me to believe that these were the same sulky, listless boys and manic dolled-up girls I had passed so often in the hallways. And it wasn't just one or two days that I saw kids out there. It was all summer long—day in and day out, two, three, or seven kids—and not just the smart kids or the ambitious kids or Sam's friends. A wonderfully motley group of kids were out there in the dirt talking, working, snacking, building something bigger than themselves.

Not one of those students including Sam, with all of his energy, could have grown those vegetables alone. The scope and ambition of the garden were essential to pulling them together. But the garden also pulled them outward toward the world.

Many of the kids who worked in the garden encountered a brand-new experience. They discovered that boring and difficult tasks like weeding could be a pleasure if those tasks led to something big— something valuable to others. Yes, the kids learned how to plant, weed, prune, and harvest. But they also learned how to actively participate in their community. They found that people who lived nearby had something to offer them and that they had something to offer in return. A Collective Endeavor should do the opposite of segregating teenagers. It should weave them tightly into society.

On a Monday morning in January, we sat down to discuss what our Collective Endeavor would be. I suspected that the conversation might take a few hours. Everyone would have a different idea of what they thought was the most important thing for us to do, and we'd have to argue it out for a while.

I was wrong.

"Well, we should do something related to education," said Mirabelle.

"Yeah, obviously," said Dominic in his high-pitched voice.

"Why obviously?" I said, surprised that two people were already in agreement about a topic, and even more surprised that it was education.

"Because," said Rix, his hat low, looking at the floor when he talked, "it's what we all care about now."

"This has changed our lives, man," said Tim. "We want other kids to be able to experience this. Hell, every kid should get to experience this."

"We should make a film," said Dakota, crouched in the corner of the room. "A documentary. About the Independent Project."

"Yeah!" said John. "Tell them how much we learned by doing things differently. Explain how important this is."

I hesitated only because I was so surprised by their overwhelming support for the idea. It had happened so quickly. "Are we sure? Should we talk about other possibilities for the Collective Endeavor?"

"Sam," said John. "You said it was supposed to have a positive impact on the broader community. I'm pretty sure the most positive impact we can have is to tell our story."

So we did. For the next three weeks, we worked on it furiously. We interviewed one another, teachers, the superintendent, the principal, Mr. Huron, even my mom. We all huddled around Tim's computer, editing it together.

"Nah, nah, nah," Dominic would say, "you should cut to Mr. Huron there."

"How about some Bob Dylan right after the blackout?"

"I really think we need someone talking about the books we read."

"Can I do my interview again?"

The best part of it all, for me, was hearing the other students give their interviews. It was like they had been storing up all this stuff to say during the semester, and with the camera on they just let it pour out. Some of them talked for more than hour. For the first time I heard Rix talk about how stupid he thought the Independent Project sounded when he first heard about it. He talked about what it was like to really learn something for the first time, to know that he knew it well, and to grapple with it on his own. Dominic, despite being camera shy, talked about the Independent Project being the only real school he had ever attended. Dakota talked about feeling challenged for the first time. I talked about coming home one day and complaining to my mom for the millionth time about how frustrated I was with school. And about how that had turned out to be the last time.

As I watched them make their film, I saw unfolding before me the unequaled impact it has on kids to feel that their work matters to others—that they can, in fact, contribute to their society. The film was a concrete way for them to express their ideas, influence others, and feel connected to a broader community—in their case an international community of students. Working on the film and knowing it would be made public had given them a sense of urgency and high standards they might not otherwise have felt. Once the film was out in the world, they got the heady reward of knowing that others heard what they had to say, took them seriously, and valued their work. A sense of social responsibility was no longer just a phrase. It was a series of actions.

We finished our fifteen-minute documentary on the last day of the semester. We celebrated as Tim uploaded it onto his YouTube account. We sent the link around to friends and family. I hoped that they would watch it and that it might change the way they thought.

And, crucially, the others hoped so too. They had stumbled into caring about their broader community. Suddenly, they found that they had something to offer—a new way to experience education—and they were scrambling to offer it.

Our friends and families did watch the film. So, it turned out, did lots of other people. E-mails starting coming in from all over the place. Hundreds of schools contacted us: a teacher in Kentucky who wanted to turn her class into an Independent Project, a principal in Australia who wanted to reshape his whole school, a fifteen-year-old in Spain who wanted to start one at his school, parents who wanted it for their kids, kids who wanted it for their friends, teachers who wanted to know how to convince principals. For the next few months, I Skyped dozens and dozens of people from all over the world. And every Skype request that came in, every e-mail that popped up in my in-box, had the same question: "How do we start our own schools?"

This book is our answer.

POSTSCRIPT

We've been wondering, recently, what we would do if we had a magic wand. Would we make traditional high schools disappear in one fell swoop, replaced by large-scale student-run schools? Actually, we're not saying that we should get rid of schools. If we had our way, IPs would not appear magically or be instituted uniformly in every school. They will be so much more powerful if they grow up organically because they're what people (kids, teachers, parents) want. That said, we think it would be great if every school had something like this. But part of the beauty and power of this idea, we think, is that the "something" will look different in each state, each town, each school—molded by the needs, demands, visions of that particular place's students. And it would be wonderful if it were more than ten kids in each school. The more high schoolers that get to experience this, the better.

Imagine a student waits for you one day after class. It might be AP English, College Prep Math, or Auto Shop. You might be the chemistry teacher, the guidance counselor, or the gym teacher. She tells you she has an idea. She might even tell you she's read this book. And she wants to start a new school. What should you do?

Make time, right away, to sit down and hear what she has in mind. Ask her to flesh out her idea—who would the school be for, how big would it be, and what kinds of things does she imagine happening each day? Avoid identifying all the obstacles ("How would you get the principal on board?" "Where would it take place?" "What about course credits?")—those obstacles are much easier to overcome once you have a clear and vivid image of the basic plan. Start by helping her think about what she wants it to be. Then you can help her figure out how to get what she wants.

Her school might look a lot like the one you've read about here. But if it doesn't, that's fine too. Each school will be different—some will have eight students, and some twenty. Some will start right off as yearlong projects, and some will not. Some will abandon math altogether and others will include it as a centerpiece. It's not important that it follows the plan of Sam and his friends. What *is* essential is that it is intellectually demanding of all its students, no matter what their academic history. It's important that the school focuses on pushing students to think rigorously and to work hard at things they care about. It is crucial that the kids have a chance to master something. It's essential that every student chooses projects, individually and collectively, that are ambitious. It's essential that, at least some of the time, the students depend on one another to learn and to make things (films, gardens, books, dinners, ideas). But whether those projects happen one after another or sequenced through the day, whether they break up into the key disciplines of sciences and languages or mesh it all together—these are the kinds of things she needs to think through.

If she hasn't done so already, help her identify some other people who will support what she is doing—other teachers, students, administrators, community members.

Most important, make time, whatever it takes, to meet with her each week, even if for only twenty minutes, so the idea doesn't get lost in the traffic of school life. Creating time and space for her to design and build her school is crucial. This is one thing most kids *cannot* achieve on their own. Students will encounter many teachers and administrators who nod at a good idea but keep thinking there's no time to do it right now—that other more urgent but less meaningful work must be attended to. Don't let urgent but unimportant work get in her way. Help her do this right now.

Once her idea has some shape to it, help her plan her next steps: support from the administration, an application process, and what kinds of things she has to figure out in the coming months. Be bold. Encourage her to make it happen the very next year. Give her suggestions. But don't take over.

Imagine your child comes home in eleventh grade and says, "I want to start a new school." First of all, jump for joy. Your daughter cares about her education and cares about other students. Best of all, she feels she can have an impact. Nurture that as if it were an orchid. You might worry about her chances of getting into college. But don't. First of all, that worry has nearly ruined our educational system. High school has become boring, tedious, unpleasant, all in the service of getting students to the next step, sacrificing a formative and potentially wonderful time of their lives for some mistaken notion that it will "get them further." It won't. A kid who is the author of her own education is more likely to thrive in every way.

Imagine a student *doesn't* come up to you one day after class. Imagine your daughter doesn't come home with an idea to start her own school. What do you do then?

Start the conversation yourself. Bring it up in your period three chemistry class. Bring it up in homeroom. Raise it with a few of your counselees. Talk about it over dinner. Ask your students, or your children, what they would do if they were in charge of high school. Ask them to envision the perfect high school. Ask them what it would look like. Make sure they realize there are no restrictions, obstacles, or limits. It's important to start there: limitless. Ask them how the periods would be broken down, what subjects they would cover, how they would learn. Maybe suggest some of the things *you* think are important, but make sure you're saying it as an equal, on level footing, not as a command. Slowly, begin to help them flesh out their ideas. Guide them, subtly, gently, making sure to step away when they push back.

Now encourage them. Say to them: why not? If they don't come to it themselves, eventually suggest that they actually do it. That they actually start their own schools. Tell them you'll be there in whatever way they need: getting other teachers on board, convincing the school committee, thinking through obstacles, designing the curriculum. But also make it clear that they need to take the lead. This is their show. Imagine that one of them finally says, "Okay, I will."

What do *we* imagine? We like to imagine that you're sixteen years old. Or maybe you've just turned seventeen. We like to imagine that you'll turn over the last page of this book, call up your best friend, and say, "I think we should start a school." Or maybe you'll tell your favorite teacher. Or bring it up at the dinner table. Maybe you won't tell anyone just yet. Maybe you're on the bus home from school. You'll just quietly slip the book into your backpack. And you'll think, "Today was the last day I'll be pissed off."

Good. You're at step one.

APPENDIX: EXTRA NUTS AND BOLTS

Below are a few specifics that weren't part of the story of the IP—but we think they might be useful to people who plan to roll up their sleeves and start a new school.

ASSESSMENT

Sam didn't think that much about assessment when he designed the Independent Project. Nor did he think that much about it *during* the Independent Project. He was so excited about making it happen, he barely stopped to wonder how anyone would know whether the project was succeeding. It was only later, when it was all over, that anyone really gave assessment any serious thought.

Given a choice between creating a really good school that educates kids well but never assesses itself, and creating a mediocre school that assesses itself all the time, the former is by far the better option. And yet, educators so often opt for the latter. When faced with an interesting idea for learning activities, or new ideas about what students should learn, people often say, "But how would you test that?" Teachers frequently choose to include things in their curricula not because they're worth doing, but because they can be easily measured.

But the truth is, the choice between a good school without assessment and a bad school with assessment is a false one. You can have a good school with assessment! And you should—for two reasons: one, some kinds of assessment improve education; they help students learn better and teachers teach better. And two, no one, no matter how great a school design they have, can know for sure that their school is doing good things unless they periodically check to find out.

Luckily, though Sam didn't think to include it in his plan, assessment was woven into the fabric of the program. First, the students used several kinds of assessment for the sake of improvement. They gave one another feedback, criticism, and judgments, all for the purpose of making each other better learners, better thinkers, and better workers. At the time it didn't appear to them to be "assessment," because, to them, "assessment" meant standardized paper-and-pencil tests and final exams.

Every Monday the IP students critiqued one another's natural and social science questions. As the semester unfolded they got better and better at criticizing one another, giving one another useful feedback, and prodding one another. Then every Friday, after one of the IP students taught the group something new, the others evaluated: research methods, materials chosen, the breadth and depth of their answers, and the degree to which they delved in. The group also evaluated one another's teaching by commenting on clarity, communication, and the use of an effective hook. Crucially, the purpose of all of that evaluating was not so that they could each get a pat on the back or a kick in the bum. They did it so that everyone would be able to improve.

Similarly, students kept two journals (one for academics and one for the Individual Endeavor) and a portfolio of their work. Keeping such records encouraged the students to regularly monitor themselves. Some kinds of learning naturally entail a lot of self-assessment. When playing the piano, for instance, it's unavoidable to hear oneself play well or badly. But with something like science, it's less natural to consistently consider whether one is learning to become a better thinker, a better scientist, or more curious. When thinking itself is what needs to improve, keeping a self-assessment journal can be very effective.

But these types of self-assessments work only if the learner is motivated to get better. People tend to take in feedback, or take advantage of self-assessment, only if they care about improving. Fortunately, in the

Independent Project, the students *did* want to improve, so the kinds of assessment they used fit their needs. Ironically, when assessment is used as a system of rewards and punishments to motivate reluctant learners, it fails because those students have little innate desire to get better at math or science or English. Instead of providing an incentive, grades become a self-fulfilling prophecy: kids become C or A students, college prep or honors, and once they've settled into such a category, things don't change much. The assessment doesn't help them get better; it just tells them how good or bad they are, have been, and will continue to be.

The IP students used a second kind of assessment for the purpose of telling other people how they were doing. This assessment was for the sake of employers, colleges, parents, and community members. It didn't contribute to the educational process the way the first kind did, but it was a required component of the school of which the IP was part.

Green River listed the Independent Project on student transcripts. On college applications, in the "additional information" box, students could include assessment letters written by Sam and Mr. Huron, which evaluated the students' work in the IP. Every college application also went out with a signed letter from the principal explaining what the Independent Project was. Many of the students wrote about their Individual Endeavors in their college essays, talked about them during their interviews, and included them on their résumés. Mr. Huron, who serves as the school's guidance counselor for college applications, believed (and heard, on occasion, from admissions officers) that the Independent Project, and the students' Individual Endeavors, made students stand out among the humdrum of honors and AP classes. It's worth noting that alumni of the Independent Project have gone on to Harvard, Wesleyan, Skidmore, Sarah Lawrence, and the University of Vermont, among other four-year institutions.

The group also used final presentations as a way to allow parents and community members to assess the IP students and the program itself. Everyone had to do a final presentation of his or her Individual

Endeavor. This was useful for two reasons. One, it allowed people to look in from the outside and judge the program and the students in it. Were the endeavors up to snuff? Did the students make real achievements in the semester? The presentations also allowed students to share their work with the public, which gave the students a concrete goal toward which to work.

When trying to write fiction, the end goal is self-evident: a complete, polished story that people want to read. But with an Individual Endeavor like learning to cook, it might be easy to drift, without having a clear destination that guides the student's day-to-day efforts. Rix's presentation was to cook a delicious four-course meal for eighty people. That gave him something to aim for from day one.

Finally, the IP students wanted to evaluate whether the Independent Project was successful. As we said at the beginning, the Independent Project could have been successful without ever being assessed. Just as there could be a great artist who never showed his work in a museum, there could be a terrific school whose success was never measured. That said, the Independent Project was part of the public school system, and for public education to work, schools need to be held to a common standard—in other words, they need to be evaluated.

Unfortunately, this is the kind of assessment Sam gave the least thought to, and we don't want others to make the same mistake. Once you've decided to start a new school, figure out what it is you want your school to achieve and how you'll measure whether or not it does that.

There were, fortunately, a few post hoc ways to measure the success of the Independent Project. One surprising way presented itself after the semester ended. Halfway through the year, students had to transition back into regular classes. There was a lot of worry among teachers about this transition. People always talked about it like it was in capital letters. What will happen after the TRANSITION? Yes, of course, but there's still the problem of the TRANSITION. Watch out for that TRANSITION!

The fear was that after a semester of the Independent Project, regular classes would be a disaster. The Indies would have forgotten how to do homework, how to listen, how to take notes, how to memorize things, and they would probably all flunk out of school. This became one of the main worries among teachers, including Mr. Huron.

It turned out it needn't have been. Almost every kid got better grades that second semester than they had in the rest of high school. Though most of them complained, when they met up occasionally to reminisce, that they found so much of it infuriatingly pointless and superficial, they also all found that the Independent Project had given them tools to make the material more interesting. They were able to pick out specific topics or ideas that caught their interest and pursue them deeply, and this, they said, accounted for their improved grades.

Needless to say, the goal of the Independent Project wasn't to make kids do better in regular school. But the fact that everyone did so well after the transition was a sign that the skills, tools, and habits they learned in the Independent Project carried over into other aspects of their lives and stuck with them. That, after all, *was* the goal. Not to learn specific information, but to learn how to learn. Doing so made them better at learning specific information once they were back in traditional school.

The success of the Independent Project can also be measured by looking at what happened during the semester. As the weeks unfolded it was easy to see that the students were engaged, that for the first time they seemed to delight in learning, reading, and working hard. The Indies talked and wrote in their journals all the time about how much they loved their new school. In the end, all they wanted to do was share their story and help other kids discover what they had experienced. With the exception of Sarah, every one of them completed an ambitious Individual Endeavor. They all talked about having discovered a new relationship to science, and every one of them either spoke or wrote about realizing what learning actually was, and feeling like they had finally become more adept it.

There's one last measure of the Independent Project's success. Dominic started a band. Rix got a job as a sous chef at one of the best restaurants in the area. John has published his writing. Sam just finished his second novel. Tim went on to make a mockumentary about high school that accrued thousands of views on YouTube. Dakota went to a top college, one famous for its writing program. None of these are explicit, standardized, objective measures. But there's no reason some of them couldn't lead to a more objective and standardized assessment.

LENGTH OF THE PROGRAM

The Independent Project should be for a year, not a semester. The nature of the program means that everything gets better with time. Doing the first Individual Endeavor is a crash course in taking ownership over something. Doing it a second time would give students a chance to hone the skills they learned the first time around. The first semester of the year, academics are really just a primer in serious thinking. That first semester gives students a chance to fall in love with learning and to get a taste for what it's like to pursue knowledge, read books for fun, and be part of a serious intellectual community. A second semester would allow students to dive deep into a few topics, developing some of the techniques that are used by serious scholars. And having more time at the end of the year for an extended Collective Endeavor would give the group a chance to do something that would have an impact on the world around them.

Here's one way to do it. Keep the first semester exactly the same, structure-wise. Then, in the second semester, have everyone do a new Individual Endeavor. This time, the only requirement would be that it's in a different field than the first one. In the second semester, eliminate the distinction between the languages and the sciences. Allow people to choose weeklong, two-week-long, monthlong academic endeavors, reading novels as a group throughout. Then allow a good five weeks for the final Collective Endeavor and have regular discussions about what it might be for the whole semester leading up to it.

It takes time to transition into being fully responsible for your own education. It takes time to build up an absorption in, and commitment to, one's Individual Endeavor. And it takes time to learn to collaborate in meaningful ways. The more time students have to do all of this, the more likely it is that they will emerge having learned things that are worthwhile and enduring.

MATH

Math was, without a doubt, the weak point of the program. In the end, the students did make progress, overcome important hurdles, and learn some lessons on the way. But even though the students started working on math and opened their minds toward it, compared to the academic triumphs in the sciences and literature, the work they did in math seemed pallid and lifeless.

We're no longer sure math should be required in the Independent Project at all. Why should every student in the IP have to learn trigonometry, geometry, calculus, and algebra? Certainly everyone should have the *opportunity* to learn those things. But lots of students don't get it, never will, and don't need to. Arithmetic, times tables, calculation, understanding of proportions are necessary for everyday life. But those should be learned before the Independent Project, before high school even. Is there anything that IP students should have to learn about math? Is there something sacrosanct about the standard high school math curriculum? The IP had already rejected the concept that there were set bodies of knowledge that all the students must learn in history, English, and science.

If math is going to be included—for example, if you're starting your new school in a state where math is required—then here are some thoughts for how it should be done. Looking back, choosing a different math topic each week was silly and pointless. At best, it gave kids a chance to discover a math topic that interested them, and perhaps reduced their fear of the subject. At worst, it reinforced the idea that math didn't interest them, wasn't relevant to their lives, and was really confusing. It trivialized mathematics.

Instead, the "math" work should be about logic and speculation, leaving numbers out of the equation as much as possible. Students could concentrate on what it means to prove something exists, logically. For instance, they might focus on why 2 + 2 is exactly the same as 4. Could it ever be any other way? They might examine what it means for two things to be equivalent, or try and understand why a set of all sets that don't contain themselves as a member is impossible. They could attempt to come up with an algorithm for finding the highest point on a foreign moon without using a map. A short, intensive course in logic could be fun for everyone, and much more helpful for high school students' mathematical understanding than learning a bunch of random math topics. This may seem like a very specific and narrow piece of advice. But it's not. It's a change that could make many more students interested in and adept at the process of mathematical thinking, without the unnecessary and often failed attempts to teach math procedures that they won't really understand and might never need again.

Math has for so long been a puzzle and a burden to teachers and students alike, and the standard efforts have resulted in little success in creating a truly numerate population. A growing number of scholars are questioning the value of teaching math as it has been taught for the past century. Doing it in a half-conventional way was a mistake for the IP. The academic integrity and impact of the program would be enhanced by the change we recommend here.

TEACHERS

So far, teachers have barely appeared in these pages. And yet, they are at the heart of education, right up there next to students, and as key to a good school's success as anything else discussed in this book. So why have we ignored them?

We haven't discussed teachers yet because Sam originally envisioned one role for them and ended up contending with a very different one. The truth is, the school wasn't able to allot the teacher hours the IP wanted. This is ironic, given that one of the faculty's biggest fears was that teachers would become irrelevant or redundant in the IP. Part of it came down to the unions. The teachers couldn't work with the IP without extra compensation, and the school didn't have enough money for that.

The upshot was that teachers had a surprisingly marginal role in the Independent Project, when they were intended to have a central role. A science, history, math, and English teacher occasionally sat in on Fridays or heard the student questions on Mondays. But that was pretty much the extent of it. Here is how they could be involved to much greater effect.

A teacher from each subject should be associated with the IP. They should serve as a source of expertise and guidance. The science and history teachers should hear everyone's questions and give feedback along with the students. They should help suggest sources, answer questions, and give guidance on research methodologies. They should engage in discussions and arguments about students' research. On Friday, they should give criticism and feedback along with the other students. And they should each choose their own question, too, and, by doing so, model how an expert does research in a given field. The English teacher should read the agreed upon books *with* students and should suggest her own. She should edit and critique the writing, join the book discussions, and read her own work aloud. The math teacher should guide the students in the core principles of mathematical thinking, like logic, as described earlier. Teachers might also invite speakers, share videos, suggest books, and offer ideas that they think might inspire students. In other words, they should provide matches to ignite the flame and add fuel once it's going.

The teachers' job in the Independent Project is nuanced and slippery. They have to guide without leading, help without pushing. They must use their judgment about when to step in and when to step back. They should use their zest for and mastery over their own subject to model how to work in that field.

This new role for teachers is much more challenging than a more traditional version. But it's also filled with less tedium, less trudging, and fewer requirements. There's more freedom for them to do their real job, which is to teach. Just as the students are free to learn any way they like, teachers would be free to help them any way they deem best. This requires a full-time investment from teachers, which the IP didn't have. But if this role is executed well, the potential for learning would shoot through the roof.

However, in a school like the IP, it's possible that even knowledgeable, wonderful teachers will find themselves helping with a topic about which they know little. A biology teacher might be asked to assist a student designing a study in genetics, for which she is woefully unprepared. An English teacher might be asked to support a student trying to interpret graphic novels, though he has never read one. What can teachers offer in cases like that? How can students apprentice themselves to teachers who are not masters of the domain in question? Here we come to one of the most potent benefits of student-run schools. We have said all along that a truly well-educated student is the one who can teach him- or herself new things. But learning how to teach yourself new things can be hard—it takes planning, ingenuity, persistence, and the ability to self-monitor. A good teacher can model good learning. Any teacher who is too worried about being asked questions to which he does not know the answer shouldn't be in a room with students. The best thing a teacher can offer is to model the process of learning new things. The teachers who are likely to be a good fit for an IP are the ones who feel confident enough in their field to tackle something unfamiliar and to make visible to the student how they go about it.

Shifting the dynamic between teachers and students is trickier than one might think. Even the teachers most committed to playing a different role can have trouble sticking with it. Recently, some teachers at Green River sent out a survey about the Independent Project, now ending its fifth year. They were looking for ways to change and improve it. Ms. Isaacs, one of the staunchest and most eloquent advocates of the IP from day one, reached out to Susan, seeking input. She explained that the program was going through a transition. Some of the teachers, it seemed, were fed up, and felt that too many of the IP students were screwing around, not taking the work seriously, or using the IP as a cover for doing whatever they wanted. She wanted suggestions for how to make the students more accountable and how to ensure that the program would once again have its former rigor. Ms. Isaacs asked, "What do you think about how the grading should be done? Should a teacher in each subject area grade the students' work each week? Do you think certain teachers should evaluate the program each year?" She listed a few other options the faculty and principal had come up with for holding the program to a high standard. Each suggestion sounded reasonable enough. But Susan couldn't help but think of the court jester in *Many Moons*. "What do the students think you should do?" she asked. Ms. Isaacs paused. "Hmm," she said. "We haven't asked them."

The most essential component of our guide is the one Sam started with. Your school must be devised by students and, with help from adults, managed by students as well. Equally important, when problems come up, and they will, it must be the students who figure out what to do. After all, it's their school.

ABOUT THE AUTHORS

Samuel Levin is the founder of two innovative, student-centered programs at his school in Massachusetts. He is a graduate of Oxford University, where he is pursuing a doctorate in zoology.

Susan Engel is a professor of developmental psychology at Williams College, where she is also the founder and director of the Williams Program in Teaching. She is the author of *The Stories Children Tell*, *Context Is Everything*, *Real Kids*, *Red Flags or Red Herrings?*, and *The End of the Rainbow* (The New Press). She lives in New Marlborough, Massachusetts.

PUBLISHING IN THE PUBLIC INTEREST

Thank you for reading this book published by The New Press. The New Press is a nonprofit, public interest publisher. New Press books and authors play a crucial role in sparking conversations about the key political and social issues of our day.

We hope you enjoyed this book and that you will stay in touch with The New Press. Here are a few ways to stay up to date with our books, events, and the issues we cover:

- Sign up at www.thenewpress.com/subscribe to receive updates on New Press authors and issues and to be notified about local events
- Like us on Facebook: www.facebook.com/ newpressbooks
- Follow us on Twitter: www.twitter.com/thenewpress

Please consider buying New Press books for yourself; for friends and family; or to donate to schools, libraries, community centers, prison libraries, and other organizations involved with the issues our authors write about.

The New Press is a 501(c)(3) nonprofit organization. You can also support our work with a tax-deductible gift by visiting www .thenewpress.com/donate.